REFLECTIONS
FROM A WOMAN
ALONE

Advance praise for Reflections from a Woman Alone . . .

"Corinne Edwards hooked me with her unabashed honesty and ever present sense of humor. This is a thoughtful and funny story of one woman's adventure in being single." —Oriah Mountain Dreamer
Author, *The Invitation*

"I love this book. I wanted more. This sometimes hilarious but always honest story proves there is no aging to the emotions of the heart—only growth toward more learning and love." —Michael F. Roizen, M.D.
Author, *RealAge* and *The RealAge Diet*

"A wonderfully humorous and courageous reflection on what many women experience at midlife." —Mona Lisa Schulz, M.D., Ph.D.
Author, *Awakening Intuition*

"Wild, hilarious, poignant, and sparklingly written, this deceptively small book packs a big and liberating punch." —Andrew Harvey
Author, *Son of Man*
and *The Direct Path*

"Courage, humor, dead-on emotional honesty, and wise compassionate observation of self and others are what distinguish this riveting story. It captures perfectly the weirdly elevated yet demeaned status of manlessness. This book is deft, immediate, and unexpectedly perfect." —Belleruth Naparstek
Psychotherapist and author, *Your Sixth Sense*
Creator of the Health Journeys guided imagery audio series

"A delightfully endearing celebration of the single woman! Through letters and poetry, you are lovingly invited inside a world that is usually kept hidden. You can learn its secrets here!"
—Judith Sherven, Ph.D., and James Sniechowski, Ph.D.
Authors, *The New Intimacy*

"Bucking an entire culture of being an unpartnered woman isn't easy; however, through her truth-telling, Corinne Edwards helps us see ourselves as the whole, full, creative beings we truly are. She gives us the courage to live out of fullness right now, no matter what." —Justine Willis Toms
Cofounder, New Dimensions Broadcasting Network
Coauthor, *True Work*

REFLECTIONS FROM A WOMAN ALONE

A Lighthearted Look at a Journey toward Wholeness

Corinne Edwards

■ HAZELDEN®

INFORMATION & EDUCATIONAL SERVICES

Hazelden
Center City, Minnesota 55012-0176

1-800-328-0094
1-651-213-4590 (Fax)
www.hazelden.org

Library of Congress Cataloging-in-Publication Data

Edwards, Corinne, 1929–
    Reflections from a woman alone : a lighthearted look at a journey
    toward wholeness / Corinne Edwards.
        p. cm.
    ISBN 1-56838-622-2
    1. Edwards, Corinne, 1929– 2. Edwards, Corinne, 1929—
    Correspondence. 3. Widows—Illinois—Chicago—Biography.
    4. Bereavement. 5. Chicago (Ill.)—Biography. I. Title.
    CT275.E3556 A3 2001
    977.3'11—dc21   00-054048

05 04 03 02 01   6 5 4 3 2 1

Author's note
This book is based on actual experiences. In some cases, the names
and details have been changed to protect the privacy of the people
involved.

Interior design by Nora Koch, Gravel Pit Publications
Typesetting by Nora Koch, Gravel Pit Publications

This book is dedicated with love and gratitude —

to my wonderful sons,
their beautiful wives—
and Veronica and Julius II

And to Dee, Julie, Pat, and Stevie,
wherever they are—
to Junie Bug
and to Jamie.

Contents

Acknowledgments

To all those who loved me and this book into actuality. Starting with my family—my sons, Mark, Paul, Peter, and Alex, their wives, Karen, Debra, and Dawn, Rain Stewart, Julius Edwards, and my precious grandchildren, Veronica and Julius II—my mother, Helen Coryat, Cecil Coryat, Henry and Isabel Coryat, June Gross, Sheila McAndrew, Gail and Bill London.

To "The Group"—Arlene Shelley, Rhea Freeman, Mary Ellen DiMatteo, Sondra Bailey, Sheila Morrison, Linda Mills, Adar Rathe, Pattie Penegor, Lee Warren, Virginia White.

To the wonderful, generous friends who support and inspire me—Ted and Patricia Kowalski, Bernie and Phyllis Curran, Katie and Stan Olson, Gail Haus, Susan Cavallo, Nora Winsberg, Ruth Warren, Linda Herrendorf, Anita Durkovic, Lee Shelley, Harriet Silver, Elma Lucas, Barbara Popovic, Joan Moloney, Ron Baker, Doug Rathe, Bob Trilling, Carole Bidnick, Penny Price, Donna Gould, Arielle Ford, James Kavanaugh, Cate Cummings, Anita Halton, Marjorie Conte, Edna Farley, Debra Goldstein, Justine and Michael Toms, Belleruth Naparstek, Marilyn McGuire, Richard Symon, Sonia Choquette, Judith Sherven, James Sniechowski, Bill Turner, Steve Juhasz, Barbara Brigel, Xavier Roy, Neale Donald Walsch, and the entire team at Wisdom Media Group.

And to those who were involved in the publishing of this book and have become friends—Gayle and Howard Mandel, June Rouse, Marilyn Allen, Bob Diforio, Karen Chernyaev, Kate Kjorlien, Jody Klescewski, Joe Riley, Karin Nord, Carol Southern, Clay Garner.

Introduction

This book seems to be about a middle-aged widow making the adjustment to single life. But it isn't. Not really. Although it opens just after my husband's death, it is not about grieving. He had been ill for many years and had suffered so much, my grief was almost all used up by the time he left. Although I missed him and was lonely and disoriented, it was a relief to let him go to a place where there was no more pain.

This is about women. Single women who are also perhaps mothers, friends, credit card jugglers, carpoolers, entrepreneurs, lovers, workers, gardeners, even grandmothers. In short, women who are trying to be everything to everybody and still have a life. I know there are some serenely, happily coupled women out there who do all of the above and do it well. If you are one of them, I don't want to exclude you. You never know when you might need a reference guide to what it's really like out there as a single woman. And male readers? Sure. Come along. It wouldn't hurt for you to learn something about how women really think.

But this for those of us who talk self-sufficiency but are furtively casting about for that guy who will defend the entrance to our cave. With all of our bravado, we are still whistling in the dark to keep ourselves safe. And no matter how successful we are, how many clothes we collect, how many pedicures we pay for, how many trips we take, how interesting our jobs, we cringe when we hear the question "Are you seeing anyone?"

Our secret is that we feel deficient without a man. We are apologetic to our families for being single. We give reasons and excuses to our friends (there's NOBODY out there). We put pieces of our lives on hold until "he" comes along.

I wasn't aware of how prevalent this kind of thinking is until my husband died. I had been married for quite a while.

This book did not start out as a collection of letters and poetry. I wrote the prologue poem, "You only get a minute./The stone has not been set/before you hear the question/'Are you seeing someone yet?'" just for fun. I could not believe that people were asking me a question like that almost immediately after my husband's death. It made me frantic. Panicky! Desperate. I had to replace this man. Plug up the hole. And I mean NOW. Don't think I am exaggerating when you read that on one sleepless night, at 3 A.M., I was counting how many men I knew whose wives were sick and were likely to die soon. Who could admit to such a shameless thing? But you see, I didn't know you were going to be reading this. I was writing for me. Kind of an exorcism. Poetry is the way I get my feelings out.

The poems grew and grew. One day I shared them with my friend Arlene. She said, "Make a book. The poems tell the inside story. Tell what is happening on the outside in your everyday life." She suggested that I share my journey in letters because everyone is an eavesdropper at heart. And there is something exciting about receiving letters. E-mail and the telephone just aren't the same.

So Arlene is to blame for this whole thing.

Will this book change your life? Are there big answers for you here? Probably not. If you are looking for a how-to book or life-changing strategies, you won't find them here. I promise you if I discover something pivotal, I'll let you know. This book is one woman's story—my story—entwined with family, friends, lovers, and assorted drop-ins. A voyage from numbness to rebirth and from confusion to some clarity—with a lot of detours! Addresses and some names have been changed and events have been altered to protect privacy. But what I found, and what you might find here, is the awareness that women, no matter what age, situation, or color, are more alike than different. There is some comfort in that.

The inspirational books we read make a thunderous announcement: No thing and no one outside us can save us. Not even a soul mate. Serenity and peace cannot be found except in our own hearts. That realization is our ultimate target. But most of us are not there yet. Glimpses—even epiphanies—come and then seem to vanish on this roller-coaster ride we signed up for. However, in between the hairpin turns and the high skydives, it's helpful to know where we are going.

If there is one message in this book, it is this: The most powerful instrument women have is our intuitive talent for nurturing, whether in our homes or our businesses. We must broaden our vistas to include more women. We need to help each other more. This is not a rally to exclude men. Bless them. We need them. But we could steal a page or two from their good ol' boy network manual.

Our experience can support a new mother who is determined to nurse a baby successfully. Our wisdom can mentor a woman who is challenged with a personal or career decision. A favor done at just the right time can make all the difference. In many instances, being present and listening are enough. The best thing about talking to girlfriends is that we permit each other's difficulties to remain unresolved. Even if we say, "Why don't you quit that job?" or, "Get rid of that jerk," we allow each other the option of taking no action on a problem. Ultimately we know what to do. We appreciate direction but don't need advice. We just need someone to hear us out.

So now, after saying that, I am going to give you some advice. No matter what your situation this minute, you can survive whatever heartbreak and loneliness you are feeling today. What they say about time healing wounds is true. But how much time you need is up to you and not some psychological calendar. It takes as long as it takes. I can't tell you at which point I started turning into myself, but it did and still is happening. It can't be hurried. Don't let anyone tell you when.

And if there is a right person—a soul mate—I believe he will show up at the perfect time, which is somehow not determined by us. We just have to follow our intuition and be alert to what is around the next bend on the roller coaster. Neale Donald Walsch, in his beautiful book *Conversations with God*, recounts that the most important question we can ask in any situation is "What would love do now?" I have those words taped on my computer screen. That guidance holds up under most circumstances. Remember to include your own happiness and welfare when you answer that question.

Some famous authors were kind enough to give me endorsements for my book. I am grateful. But comments from women, ordinary people like you and me, are also encouraging. Linda, who is thirty-eight, said, "It's all here. I laughed. I cried." Dawn, twenty-nine, wrote, "I could not put this book down." And Susan, forty-eight, called to say, "I thought you had been reading my mail!" Different ages. Different situations. We are all writing the same story.

Thanks for listening to my story. You may find some of your mail here. I hope it will make you know you are not alone. My mother's favorite expression was "In the light of all Eternity, most things don't matter." She was probably right but the events in our lives sure feel important today. Even if things don't really matter, go for the gold anyway! Every way you can. And every day. You are a beautiful, extraordinary woman—with or without a man. And you have a unique contribution to make to yourself and to your world.

Prologue

You only get a minute.
The stone has not been set
before you hear the question
"Are you seeing someone yet?"

You have not filed the insurance,
transferred a single bond
before they sing the litany
"Remember, life goes on."

It's not the lonely evenings
that strike terror in your breast.
It's the envelopes that come addressed
to "Ms. You and your guest."

The dilemma's not in grieving
or even what to wear
but where you find a body
to escort you to affairs.

They say you're far too fussy.
There is nothing much out there.
They use as their criteria
if a man can breathe and stare.

I'd run away to Tonga,
Abu Dhabi, or Tibet,
but I know that someone there would ask
"Are you seeing someone yet?"

If you find yourself a widow,
start wailing right away.
You only get a minute
before you have to play.

Gone

Dear Sheila,

Wish I could just pick up the phone and call you, but Kuala Lumpur is a long way away. So I'll just tell you the news.

My husband, Julie, died. It finally happened.

I am taking some comfort in the fact that he died at home with all of us around him—even the dog.

He put up a heroic fight, but it started to really go downhill right after Christmas. The cancer had spread to his spine and he couldn't walk. A lot of pain. Morphine, the whole bit. I want to tell you, by February, I was praying for him to die. The doctor said he probably weighed about seventy pounds, and you know what a big man he was.

Things have been kind of in a blur ever since.

Believe it or not, I gave him a Jewish funeral. You know how he always hated being Jewish. Well, about two weeks before he died, he said, "I know I have never been a good Jew, but I want to be buried as a Jew anyway. Just don't get one of those rabbis with the curly sideburns to do it." I hope he was there watching from wherever people go when they die. He would have been very surprised and satisfied with the arrangements for his funeral.

I found a rabbi from London. Complete with British accent. Graduated from Oxford. Clean shaven. Central casting at Universal could not have done it better. It was a classy funeral. The rabbi gave a eulogy like he had known Julie for life, and he only spoke to us for fifteen minutes before the service.

So it is all over. My sister June stayed with me for a couple of weeks, which was a big help, but she had to go back to her family. The older boys went back to California where they share an apartment. Peter is playing lead guitar in a rock band, and Paul is working for a video production company. So it is Alex and me here alone. He is starting college soon and life is going on.

I went back to work in the travel agency. Not exactly the soul satisfaction you must have with your assignment in the peace corps, but it is something to do and I need the routine. The other distraction I have is that I decided to settle the estate matters myself. I am up to my ears in paper. I am finding out that it is very complicated to die. I do ask for accounting and legal help as I need it, but a lot of the work in filing insurance forms, transferring stock, car, real estate, etc., is just busy work. Sometimes I don't know what I am applying for when people like those in the Veterans Administration send me mysterious forms. But I just keep filling things out and mailing them back.

A death makes you face your own mortality. And it makes everyone else conscious of it too. My sons were sitting around a few days after we buried him—God bless them, they didn't realize what effect it was having on me—and they started talking about which art in the house they would finally inherit. I felt as though I was at my own will reading.

Being a widow makes me feel like I've been neutered. I didn't realize how uncomfortable people feel toward you when you don't have a man. It has been only two months, and already several of my clients—I mean, really sweet, well-meaning, kind people—have asked me if I am seeing anyone yet. I've been in a state of shock about that. The man is not cold. A friend who is a decorator is already talking about what color flowers I should have on the tables for my next wedding and where it should be. It makes me feel panicky. Suddenly I am half a person. Why do we feel like we are incomplete without a man?

There have been several invitations to weddings and parties and every envelope is addressed to me "and guest." I'm still hemorrhaging, and I feel like I have to look for a date so I don't upset table arrangements!

The world doesn't seem to give much time for recovery.

Sure wish you were not so far away. Miss you. Especially now.

Write to me.

Love,
Corinne

Dearest Paul and Peter—

I'm glad that you two are settled back into your apartment and your jobs. I know how difficult it was for you when you had to leave me and Alex here in Chicago, but we had to face the future sometime without your support and we are starting to do that. It is funny that even the absence of stress and worry leaves a big void. There are spaces in the day now that we don't yet know how to fill. I keep trying to remember what I did with my time before so much of it was taken up with one medical crisis after another.

In the years ahead, you will think about some of the last events of your dad's illness and be very consoled by the compassionate and tender way you cared for him in his last weeks. You did every possible thing for him—physical and mental—that could be done. There are not too many sons who would leave their lives and their careers for a month to be with their father in his last days.

I keep thinking about what he said to you the day before he died. He called the two of you into the room to tell you, "I'm sorry. You know, I just never understood you boys. But you were never wrong. You were just different from me."

Later in the day, he held his hands together and said, "The boys and me. We are tight, tight, tight."

Those last moments signified great emotional healing for him and for you in your relationship. There was no more talk about your getting a "real profession." He realized that neither of you would be an accountant or a doctor and that you are just fine the way you are. That final acceptance and love will console you throughout your life every time you think of him.

I cannot ever thank you enough for the comfort it gave Alie and me to have you (and your sturdy backs) here with us. Alex keeps talking about how you stopped him, Peter, as he was leaving the house for his senior play rehearsal, and you said, "Alie, take off your coat. Stay home today. Don't go." None of us knew that day would be Dad's time to leave, but somehow, at some level, you did, Peter. Alex would have always regretted not being there for that last peaceful moment in Dad's life.

We have always been a close family, but this sadness has woven an even stronger bond than we ever had before. I am so grateful for all of you. We all seem to be more grateful for each other.

This is a big adjustment period. But you know what? We're doing it—and we're going to make it! Just the way Dad would want us to.

Alex and I both send our love. And I want you to know I am so proud to be your . . .

Mom

Six-Week Checkup

Psychologists say
when you lose a mate,
it takes six weeks
to even feel it.

They are wrong.

When you are fully prepared,
intelligent, stable,
super-efficient,
have advice from a lawyer,
accountant, and broker—
you file the papers,
mail the forms,
transfer the car—

3 A.M.
an acre of bed
out of cigarettes
ice cream gone
eating chocolate
dogs are barking
find a man
getting older

car is stalling
roof is leaking
bills are piling
find a man
have a party
buy a condo
diet center
find a man
start a business
foreign travel
have an eyelift
find a man
a new wardrobe
join a health club
list the sick wives
find a man
tally assets
count your contacts
singles dances
find a man
find a man
find a man

Steins Funeral Home
4433 West State Avenue
Chicago, IL 60659

Dear Mr. Stein:

I want to thank you again for the lovely arrangements you made for my husband's funeral in March.

However, I was more than a little surprised to find your additional bill for $600 in my mail today.

You may remember that when you were selling us a casket, I was quite clear that we did not need to purchase a more expensive one because it had a "younger look." My husband was a very conservative man and, in addition, was already pretty old when he died.

Also, I did not feel that the extra half inch of Styrofoam, which was a feature of your deluxe model, would contribute very much to his eternal rest.

You may remember that, since I was under great stress, I could not stop laughing in your casket room for a half hour. Therefore, I am certain you will have no difficulty in recalling our transaction and will correct your records accordingly.

Again, thank you for all your consideration.

Sincerely,
Corinne Edwards

June 15

Veterans Administration
2625 Milwaukee Avenue
Chicago, IL 60618

Dear Sir or Madam:

Thank you for sending me the sixty pages of forms. I have filled them out to the best of my ability.

I don't know my husband's date of discharge because it was before I knew him. But he was in your Navy, so you must have it somewhere.

I have one question about all this. What am I applying for?

Sincerely,
Corinne Edwards
(Mrs. Julius Edwards)

July 11

Veterans Administration
2625 Milwaukee Avenue
Chicago, IL 60618

Re: Your file 69421835890

Dear Sir or Madam:

I knew all along my late husband was not disabled in a war, so I am not disappointed that I am ineligible for a pension.

The other reason you have denied my request (of which I am not entirely clear) is that my income is over your limit and exceeds $170,000 per year.

I would very much appreciate it if you would tell me where you have found that income in case my husband neglected to inform me of it.

Anxiously awaiting your reply.

Sincerely,
Corinne Edwards
(the legal widow of Julius Edwards)

August 10

Supervisor of Benefits for Veterans
Veterans Administration
2625 Milwaukee Avenue
Chicago, IL 60618

Re: Your file 69421835890

Dear Sir or Madam:

I am really annoyed, actually enraged, by the gross ineffi-
ciency of a department that I and my entire family have
been paying taxes to for many years.

First you made me fill out sixty pages of forms with no
explanation as to why or what I was applying for. Then you
turn me down because of lack of disability in the service
and too much income.

Now you write to tell me that I qualify for nothing, after
all this effort, because I have income of over $4,200 per year.
Would you mind telling me where the other $165,800 that
you previously found went?

I have called your office repeatedly about this matter and
no one seems to know what I'm talking about. I have a
right, as an American citizen, to claim money that you have
determined belongs to me.

If I do not hear from you immediately, I shall turn this
matter over to my attorney.

Sincerely,
Corinne Edwards
(the LEGAL widow of Julius Edwards)

MCBRIDE, COKER AND KLEIN
ATTORNEYS-AT-LAW
600 WEST LA SALLE STREET
CHICAGO, IL 60606

September 16

Mrs. Corinne Edwards
6400 North Lincoln Avenue
Lincolnwood, IL 60646

Dear Mrs. Edwards:

Thank you for entrusting your grievance against the Veterans Administration with our firm.

After an exhaustive search, there seems to be no basis to your allegation that they have hidden information from you on money which is rightfully yours. The letter from them, which you sent for our records, does not appear in your file at all. It is possible that your name was mistakenly placed on that correspondence.

We did have a conversation with the supervisor about this matter, and he has promised to advise his staff to be more careful in the future. He expressed his apologies for your distress.

Our invoice for $350 is enclosed.

We are looking forward to representing you in the future.

Sincerely,
Sally James
Paralegal for Henry McBride

Dear Marion,

Your letter was so comforting. And I want to especially thank you for your contribution to the American Cancer Society.

I am doing pretty well. Of course, it is a big adjustment. But when you see someone in the condition my husband was when he died, you wouldn't have him back like that for a million dollars.

The kids are doing fine. Paul and Peter live in Los Angeles. Alex is still at home (when he's home) attending college. Their lives go on as usual. And I have a travel agency to run, so that keeps me busy. I have also joined a spiritual (not religious!) support group that helps. It's all about loving yourself and other people, which wouldn't do any of us any harm.

It would be nice to see you when I take a trip back east. Let's plan on it.

Love,
Corinne

P.S. You remember Sheila. We've been in touch. You may have heard that her son died tragically. After that, she joined the peace corps because she said she was sick and tired of making more money in her advertising agency for already rich people. Julie and I saw her a couple of years ago when we were on a trip to Malaysia. She is working with children using her communication and theater background, and it is very satisfying to her. It's nice to stay in contact with our old friends. We need each other.

Pussycat Love

Sarah Mae Pussycat,
also known as
The Queen of the Universe,
attends our weekly support group meetings.

She arrives in a cardboard box,
her bright eyes dim,
whiskers tattered,
once beautiful coat
hanging dull on her body,
and lies still.

Even my Doberman,
who normally takes exception
to this natural enemy,
doesn't seem to mind.

The lady she lives with
takes her everywhere now.
She is very ill.
No one should die alone.
And she hasn't seen much,
having been a house-type cat.
What wisdom can you take away

if you have viewed the world
from a windowsill?

Windowsills.
We sit on our windowsills.
Watching out through cloudy glass.
Peering through our drapes.
Afraid to go out, take chances.
Putting life off, sure we have time,
while our cells sign off, quietly,
one by one.

Aren't we all critical cases?

Our meetings revolve around unconditional love,
giving, and the gift of receiving,
accepting ourselves and others
just the way we are,
and, on nonattachment,
loving and letting go.

As we review these principles,
our eyes shift often
to a silent cardboard box.

Sarah Mae Pussycat,
The Queen of the Universe,
did not attend this week.

Dear Junie Bug,

I can't wait! A whole week in New York! It seems like forever since we've been together, and the last time was certainly not very happy. Our "Big Apple Experience" is really needed this year. Tell Doug he is the best brother-in-law in the world to let me have you all that time.

I am enclosing a check for the theater tickets. They sound like fun, but be prepared—I am going to shop! Not only have I not bought anything new in ages but everything in my wardrobe reminds me of Julie. You know how fussy he was about what I wore.

I feel like I want to change everything. I am trying to be me. Wish I knew who that was.

See you very soon!

Love you,
Corinne

Best Intentions

On the plane to New York,
I decided to

- quit smoking
- love everyone unconditionally
- stop interfering with my children
- be nonjudgmental
- keep my old car
- sell my business
- meditate daily
- learn to do channeling
- find a lover
- get married
- lose five pounds
- pay off my Visa and cancel the card
- get the latest books on cassettes
- travel more
- make new friends
- donate time to charity
- listen to my body
- give up sugar permanently
- join Toastmasters
- buy a concert series
- sign up for a writing course

- increase my business
- exercise every day

When the plane landed in New York,
all I thought about was

Bloomingdales.

Gone

He is gone.
Only a wisp of his presence remains.
An unfinished life,
the look of wonderment on his face
when he first held his son,
pipes on a shelf,
cuff links from Italy,
a family laughing by a Christmas tree.

They shipped his things from the office.
Forty years in a small box.
It was a transitory joining,
the years, an instant in time.

At the end
I tried to heal for him,
make it right, stop the pain,
do it for him, carry him.

but he carried his,
and I carry mine

He is memories.
A dark blue Lincoln.

Begonias in the basement for the winter.
Japanese fish in a pond.
September Song.

he is gone

Alie, are you in there?

Yes.

Would you come out a minute? I want to talk to you.

What do you want?

Look, I want to apologize for what I said. I realize that you meant well when you told me that you were paying all the bills in the house from now on. It was mean of me to say that you could pay the bills when you bring in the money. I'm just under a lot of stress. I'm not myself lately.

I thought it would help you if I did what Dad did.

I know, Alie. But, there's plenty of time for you to have those responsibilities in the future. But not now. You don't have to pay the bills. I can do it.

I wouldn't mind doing it.

I know you wouldn't. But it isn't necessary. And another thing, Alie. I don't want you to think you have to stay home and keep me company. I want you to go out with your friends like you always have.

I don't want you to be alone, Mom.

Please, Alie. I want you to be a kid. Just be a kid. That would help me the most. I'm doing fine. Just be a kid. Please. And I'm very sorry I spoke to you that way.

I love you, Mom.

I know. And I love you. Very much.

Loyola University
Bursars Office
Lake Shore Campus
Chicago, IL 60618

Re: Alexander Edwards
Student #369270670

Dear Sir or Madam:

I received your bill for my son's second semester tuition today, and I was alarmed to see that it has gone up already.

I know you have a six-month budget plan, but I was wondering if you have any kind of a special twenty-year plan? Something like a mortgage?

Please advise.

Corinne Edwards

Think Tank

My son, the college student,
interrupts my Sunday *Times*
reading long paragraphs from *Walden,*
and contends
that studying the great philosophers
could benefit
even my mundane
and generally pointless existence.
Besides, he says,
I could think a lot more.

He's probably right.

But, Commonwealth Electric
has never heard of Nietzsche.
They believe in good and evil.
Don't know from things eclectic,
and get stern when I've suggested
my payment's not reflected
since their meter is defective.

He chides me almost daily
that trips sold to Miami,
charters to Las Vegas,

and cruises to Hawaii
contribute nothing to my rapture.
I'm confused when this is followed by:
I have no human nature.
There's no God to even think me.
(Sartre is this week's chapter.)

He spends hours in the library
intent on metaphysics,
studies fundamental values,
Aristotle's ethics,
and I could spend my evenings better
than books on self-improvement,
and guides which guarantee a lover
if followed to the letter.

He writes reams on his computer,
thoughts IBM compatible,
explores Plato's Theaetetus,
like I talk about the weather.
While directly on their statement,
I scribble to my banker
for applications for a loan
to fix my leaky basement.

He is tortured by the choosing,
Aquinas or Suzuki.
Is it faith and hope and charity

or is Zen the more shibui?
While I grapple with decisions—
Replace the dryer motor?
Is blue the perfect color
for the chair and for the sofa?

While I'm soaking in the bathtub
bombarding all my senses
with subliminal recordings
(my Creating Money lessons),
my son, the college student,
is running with the muses,
looking for the meaning,
reaching to solutions,
searching out the answers—

I've run out of excuses.

Could you please repeat the question?

Dear Junie Bug,

The weather is beautiful in the Caribbean! I wish I could report that I'm having a glorious time.

This ship is full of widows. Funny, although I've been on a lot of ships, I never noticed so many before. I guess because I wasn't one of them before.

I decided I would pretend that there is me, and then, all of them. We are not connected. But I would make a study to see what widows do. Start to educate myself for some future trip.

This is the way it looks.

They are busy. Maybe that's the way to defer loneliness. They are organized. They plan things to have a good time. Many of them seem to know each other from other trips, and they have routines. They plan cocktail parties, meet for bridge games, operate ten bingo cards at one time. Shopping is an art form. They have lists of exactly what they are going to buy in each port and in which store and precisely what they are going to pay.

The worst part of it is that they really seem to be enjoying themselves. They are actually having a lot of fun together!

June, I hate this. I hate being a widow. I don't like not having a partner.

I met a lovely woman on deck who is also alone. She said I'd get used to it. That I would make a life for myself without a man. She said I had to. I must.

I suppose she's right. But do I have to get started right now? I'm not ready yet.

Going away alone so soon was a big mistake.

I can't wait to go home to my house and my big chair and my office—and to Alie. I'm safe there.

Love you,
Corinne

Lost at Sea

We ring the dance floor,
battalions of widows
in sequined dresses
the lady at Saks
guaranteed
would enflame any man's passion.

We sit in formation,
heckling the magician
after a dinner of 5,000 calories,
where we listed our ships,
counted destinations,
and bragged of the bargain
on camel seats that day.

Four bachelors
(a retired sock salesman,
a prostate operation recoveree,
and two elderly gay men)
plus three exhausted cruise directors
and a few resentful officers
are the prizes for the evening.

The score kept on the voyage
is not who wins at bingo,
finds the most jade jewelry,
or is sleeping with the captain,
but who gets the most dances.

A sea of sailing women
armed with sequined dresses,
collecting foreign cities,
buying Turkish carpets,
spending the insurance,

when all we ever wanted
was a condo on the ocean
and a trailer trip cross-country
with the man who paid the premiums.

Dear Paul and Peter—

Alex is so excited since you helped him get a job as a guide at Universal Studios this summer! It will be such a nice change for him to get away from Chicago and be with you. I hope your apartment won't be too crowded with the three of you, but I know you'll all have fun together.

I am enclosing a check to help defray the cost of extra food for the first month. Let me know if you need more. That kid can eat! I don't want his visit to be a financial hardship on your household.

I'm so glad to hear that things are going well with the music and video production out there. I'm sure that Alex will enjoy all the excitement of your lives in Los Angeles! He has gotten so serious about studying philosophy! He could use a little lightening up!

Try not to fight!

I love you all.

Mom

Dear Sheila,

Thank you so much for your beautiful letter. Please don't apologize for taking so long to write. I understand it sometimes takes time for letters to reach you.

Yes, I am remembering the good things. We did have a wonderful time when we saw you in Malaysia two years ago. It still makes me laugh when I think of how we sneaked you on that bus as a travel agent on the familiarization tour. The hotel people were so impressed that an agent from Chicago could speak the language!

My life seems to be in limbo. It's very quiet in the house. Alex is spending the summer in Los Angeles with his brothers. He got a job as a guide at Universal Studios. It is a big adjustment to be alone. Seven P.M. and weekends are the worst time. Everyone you know is having dinner and you sit there alone. The worst of the worst are Sunday afternoons! During the week, I manage pretty well because I'm at the travel agency and I love the clients who come in, but it's getting harder and harder to push myself out the door to get there. I have lost interest in most things. I feel frozen.

There is another big adjustment I didn't anticipate. I hope this doesn't sound like a dirge to you. But not being part of a couple has excluded me from my whole social world. For example, a friend tried to be very diplomatic about why she was not inviting me to her dinner party. She explained that her table sat ten persons. If she asked me, there would only be nine and it eliminated her opportunity to include another COUPLE to whom she owed an invitation. If I were part of a twosome, she wouldn't have to waste a chair.

And this is almost funny, if it didn't hurt. All of a sudden I have become a threat—some kind of a siren—as a single woman. When I am included in a gathering, I have to be very careful not to spend too much time talking to other women's mates. They don't like it. It was okay when I had a man there, but it is not okay now. And believe me, some of these men I am supposedly trying to seduce wouldn't tempt me if we were on a desert island for ten years!

Thank God for Snoopy. Do you remember how I vehemently protested having such a big dog in the house? He's become my best friend. And he doesn't ever exclude me from his love! He is always delighted to see me.

I hope your production of *Anything Goes* is wildly successful. I can just see all those little Malaysian faces singing "You're the Top!"

Keep writing when you can.

Love,
Corinne

P.S. Speaking of Alex, he has changed his major from business administration to, of all things, philosophy. He told me he wants to study something that will help him his whole life. I am inclined to agree, but I bet his conservative father is spinning in his grave about it!

Editor
Travel Agent Monthly
666 North Main Street
Philadelphia, PA 12045

Dear Sir:

I was reading your article *Seven Sure Steps to Hammer That Vacation Sale Home,* which appeared in your April issue, when I happened to overhear Margie, one of our salespeople, greet a client in the front office.

That was when I realized how out of touch you people are up in your ivory tower of publishing. You don't have a clue about what goes on in the neighborhood travel agency.

To give you an idea of what really happens, I am enclosing a transcript, almost word for word, of what a client said to my colleague. Margie said very little during the sale, and that was what was called for.

To the casual observer, it does not seem like this is a sale, but I guarantee you that this woman will come back and book with us. She always does. Besides, I defy you experts to "hammer" this client about anything.

On your list, you left out two very essential sure steps: CARING and LISTENING.

These human ingredients cannot be found on the Internet or in the tricks you suggest in your article.

Sincerely,
Corinne Edwards
President

"So I Said to Shelley . . ."

A Travel Sale

"Margie! It's so great to see you! You look terrific. I came in to talk to you because I wanted to go to Canada. Shelley and I have been talking about it. It sounds terrific. But I don't know what to do. I talked to Shelley and he said, well, it's the money you know and I said, listen, you've been working hard all year. You know. He's a sick man, Shelley. Shelley's a very sick man. And I mean, I said to Shelley, if he didn't smoke he wouldn't have those circulation problems. We went to the store the other day and I said, Shelley, sit down. Sit down, Shelley. You look terrible.

"Anyway we want to go to Canada, and Linda came over the other night and she said, Ma, go to Canada. It would do you both good. You know my daughter Linda. Well, she got so beautiful. You met her. I mean, I can't understand it. I mean, thirty-three. I don't know what she's looking for. I said to her, Linda, I don't care if you are happy. You got to get married. And I said to Shelley, that's a girl. She says, go to Canada.

"So we're thinking about what we should do. I don't know if we should go straight to Toronto. I don't know. Quebec is nice. What do you think? My friend, she said, go to Quebec. It's terrific. She said, stay in the Chateau

Frontenac. But you have to be careful. She said it's a terrific place but you can get in a closet.

"You remember last time we went to Boston. You gave us that room for $55. And I said to the woman, I said, listen, I want to be up where I can see the river, and she said for the river she gets $85. And I said no river's worth it to me. So we stayed in the room for $55. What do I care? I mean you look at a river. You look at a parking lot. But on the way back, when we stayed there again, I said, how about the river? And she said, you got it. For $55 she gave me the river.

"But getting back to Canada. I don't know the date. I'm not sure if we can leave on the fourteenth or the twenty-fourth. I said to Shelley, Shelley, make up your mind. Shelley, talk to your boss. Find out. When is your vacation anyway?

"Do you need a date to book it? I mean, couldn't you call them? You'll tell them, look, she doesn't know. She's either coming on the fourteenth or the twenty-fourth. We don't know yet. She has to talk to her husband and he's got to talk to his boss so we don't know.

"Anyway, I'm going home. I'm cooking. I don't have to. Shelley doesn't make me cook. But I said to Shelley, I'd rather go out to a terrific place once a week than every night to a nothing.

"But I'm glad we got this all set up now. Shelley will be happy. I'll tell him what we did. And we'll see what Shelley thinks."

You just made an illegal left turn. Didn't you see that sign?

No, I'm sorry, officer, I didn't.

That sign is as big as a house, lady. You women drivers!

I'm sorry. I didn't see it.

Do you know your license plate expired four months ago?

No.

And your city sticker expired two months ago?

No. I didn't realize it.

What is it with you, lady? Do you know I'm going to have to give you three tickets? Why didn't you take care of these things?

Men do these things with cars. I'm sorry, but my husband died. He always took care of the cars.

Well, I'm sorry to hear about your husband, but you're the one who is going to have to show up in court. You're going to have to get it together, lady.

Okay. I will.

Look, this is none of my business, but I notice these things. According to the sticker on your car, you haven't changed the oil in 6,000 miles. You should take care of that.

Thanks for telling me. I will.

And start looking at signs.

Okay.

Mr. Henry McBride
McBride, Coker and Klein
Attorneys-at-Law
600 West La Salle Street
Chicago, IL 60606

Dear Henry,

Thanks for the invitation to your party. Sincere congratulations on your new life as senior partner in your firm!

It will be with great pleasure that I will be there to celebrate with you.

Henry, I know I've said this to you in person, but I want to tell you again how much your support meant to all of us during Julie's long illness. We could not have made it without you.

So many things helped. The time you went to Alex's school play. The Saturday visits to bring fresh fish when Julie would eat nothing else. How patient and kind you were when he got so cantankerous.

Most of all, thank you for your constancy. I know you said it was "enlightened self-interest," but to us it seemed like you invented the word *friendship*. We always knew you were just a phone call away.

See you on Wednesday! As they say, I'll be there with bells on!

Fondly,
Corinne

Miscasting

It was a fabulous party,
a hundred guests,
the movers, the shakers,
tossed with enough
art, music, and theater eccentrics
to make it sparkle,
and I felt so lonely.

Brittle repartee,
extravagant food,
beautiful people,
a jazz quartet in the background,
and I felt so lonely.

My dress was a smash,
hair, makeup perfect.
I listened and laughed,
charmed with the best
at hit-and-run conversation,
and I felt so lonely.

I felt as though
there was a plate-glass wall
between me and the party.

I was watching myself on the stage
outside it.

There was not one person in the cast who loved me,
and I felt so lonely.

Reunion Committee

Enclosed is my check for $30 for the reunion dinner. The plans sound like it is going to be a lot of fun.

I am glad the name tags will also include our original class picture. That way we will definitely know who we are talking to!

Can't wait to come home!

Sincerely,
Corinne Edwards

Dear Sheila,

I know that you are sometimes out of civilization, but it has been a long time since I have heard anything from you. Where have they put you? Please let me know when you can.

I'm going to write until you do. It does me good to get my thoughts on paper. And mail them so far away. Kind of an exorcism.

I regret to report that the news here is not good again. My closest friend, Anne, is very ill. Cancer again. They are giving her a matter of months. To make things worse, she also works in the office as my bookkeeper. So I am trying to handle the personal loss and also look for a new staff member.

What really makes me sad is how she saved money and deprived herself of so many things she wanted in case of a "rainy day." The rainy day is here and she'll end up with a nice estate, but she missed a lot of pleasure. The only consoling thought is that I convinced her, in the past few years, to take advantage of some of her profession's travel benefits. She traveled with her brother, who is a priest, and justified spending the money to give him the opportunity to see the world. Otherwise she lived poor. They will never say that about me. If I have it, I spend it. I'll probably end up a bag lady.

Last week I went to my class reunion. I'm not going to say how many years. (Why would I lie to you? You already know.) It was a shock to see how old those high school faces got. I pulled out all my finery to try to look good, but they are probably saying the same thing about me.

It was nice to see everyone but I felt so disconnected. Most of them still live where I grew up. They are such country people, but you know, they seem so happy.

Where do I belong? I feel like everything is draining away. I don't feel at home here. I don't live there anymore.

I confess, I thought you were a little nuts to close up a successful advertising agency and join the peace corps. I know you were devastated when your son died, but it seemed like such an extreme step. Now I envy what you are doing. You have a purpose. My boys are grown. There seems no role for me now. Worse, I have no role and I don't seem to have the energy to want one.

Wish you were closer. Write when you get this.

Love,
Corinne

Going Home

So many years had passed,
but only a few had moved away
from my high school town.
They were fascinated I had flown
all that way for just a day
to the reunion.

The same people. Still there.
Fatter, thinner, balding, bifocaled.
Time had scribbled unkindly
on some of the faces.
They had married each other.
The football team.
The majorettes.

They spoke of local politics,
names I didn't recognize,
complained of the traffic on Main Street now
since the city people moved up,
were still debating the grade
Mrs. Moffit gave them in geometry.
Their kids play on the same teams.
They married each other too.

They clapped when a letter was read.
The class braggart couldn't make it.
Two discs had been removed.
More applause.
Everything he had bragged he would do,
he had done.

The boy most likely to succeed
read meters for the gas company,
the peppiest died on skid row,
the most intellectual, when his wife left the room,
asked me to dinner.
He had always wanted to date a cheerleader.

In my Italian silk dress,
an exercised size eight,
wearing a ring I acquired in Sydney,
earrings discovered in Nice,
I was an alien, a UFO
Although I'd been a great dancer,
no one asked me to dance.

The trees on the mountains
were flaming red
as I drove to the airport,

so beautiful,
my heart hurt.

But, they were not my trees anymore.

It was not my town.

Dear Paul and Peter and Alex—

Thanks so much for the telephone calls and especially the birthday cards that arrived right on time! I loved all the personal notes you included. It sure makes a mom feel loved and wanted!

It was also nice to hear you don't need any more money to help with Alex's room and board. Wow! You guys are really learning to manage well.

I notice that Dr. Greene's dental bills are no longer arriving. Could it be that you paid them? (Another "Wow!" if this is so.)

All is well here. Snoopy and I are enjoying the summer.

Love to you all,
Mom

P.S. Alex, if you are homesick, just COME HOME! In the light of all eternity, a job at Universal Studios is not that important. I miss you too.

Dearest Junie Bug—

I can't wait for you to come! Although Chicago is not up to our "Big Apple Experience," there are lots of things to do here. I am enclosing the "Arts and Entertainment" section of the *Tribune* so we can confer on what you'd like to see, and of course you can always enjoy the Art Institute of Chicago. And we can SHOP!

I am sorry to say my friend Anne is not responding to the chemotherapy. She seems to have given up. She is no longer coming in to the office at all. We'll have lunch when you come. Maybe it will cheer her up. I wish I knew what to do to make things better for her.

It is sure quiet in the house since Alex left for California. He sounded a little homesick at first but that seems to have passed. It is nice for him to spend some time with his brothers—the odd couple, as Julie used to call them—in Los Angeles.

The boys are really growing up. For one thing, they are starting to understand that Mom's "bank" is closed and are becoming financially responsible. That is a shock. I must admit that I did help them with an emergency transmission job a few months back, but other than that, things have definitely changed.

For example, I no longer get the dentist bills—and they got their own credit cards in their own names!

And birthday and Mother's Day cards arrive on time! No more excuses about the rotten post office, being out of stamps, or their corner mailbox being hit by a truck!

I hear Peter has taken over the finances of their household. Interesting that he is the one who looks wild—with the long, blond, rock-and-roll hair—a real out-there people person—but he pays the bills and has his feet squarely on the ground. I told someone the other day that if I got arrested in Singapore, I'd call Peter. He'd figure a way to get me sprung!

Paul, on the other hand, with his quiet nature and GQ looks, is quite oblivious to such mundane and nonessential matters as rent, buying groceries, or paying the electric bill. He operates in his own world, intent on doing the things he wants to accomplish and loves to do.

Julie was right. They really are the odd couple!

I guess I like the older boys being independent. My checkbook balance looks better at the end of the month. I just have my sweet Alie to support in school now.

But I am trying to figure out why I am starting to feel a little unnecessary.

We'll brainstorm this and other momentous problems of world affairs when you arrive.

Hurry! I'm lonesome.

Your devoted sister,
Corinne

Dearest Anne,

Even though we have known each other for twenty years, it is hard to say in person the things I have in my heart.

So, with this letter, I am putting a poem I wrote about you in your mailbox today. I want to share some of the feelings I have about you and this terrible illness.

We sure have had our ups and downs over the years. A lot of fun and some bad misunderstandings. I have been thinking lately about the year we didn't speak because of that stupid mix-up about what time we were to get together Christmas Day. I've been wishing we had that year back. I could use it now.

We've gone through so many things together. I don't know how I would have gotten through my husband's death without your support. And how can I thank you enough for taking over the entire funeral lunch and the cleanup? You are my rock and my rudder. And I am also trying to remember all the laughing! When all the pieces are put together, we have had a major friendship.

I hope what I have written will not make you feel bad. That is not my intention. As a matter of fact, if you could possibly heal and get well, that would be my dearest wish. Try for me, if for no other reason—I may go bankrupt without you yelling at me about my spending!

I just want to express how precious the time with you has been.

Love always,
Corinne

Best Friend

You're leaving, my friend.
The doctors agree.
They have dotted the i's,
slashed all the t's.
Your name is inked in blood.

I am trying to console myself.
You have always been happiest
when you're going on a trip.
But you won't come home this time.

They won't even let me plan it.
Not qualified.
I don't remember the destination,
or know the visa requirements.
The routing to heaven
is not in my computer.

The new travel agent is your Jesus.
I hope he knows what he's doing.
Tell him nonstop—not direct
(that's an old airline trick),
and you're used to flying first class!

Be very specific about your accommodations.
The pretty house,
an Oriental rug with a lot of blue in it,
shutters in the windows, the country kitchen,
your own big bathroom, crown moldings, paneled doors.
All the things you never had.
You deserve it. Show them your record.

About your trip to China,
I think that can be negotiated.
Say it's been planned.
You've saved up for it.
There's got to be a way
to get to China from there.

You're leaving, my friend,
and I'm not being a good sport about it.

Instead of remembering
all the years,
I am holding on to every moment,
memorizing words you say,
locking in your every glance,
begging time to tell you
over and over,
how much I love you,
how much I'll miss you.

The tears on this page will dry.
I'll know you're finally out of pain,
your struggle over,

but for now, my friend,
all I feel is abandoned.

you are leaving

Dear Sheila,

Yes, this letter is from me! You must have wondered when you saw the postmark from Athens.

Anne's funeral was beautiful. Hundreds of people came. Her brother—the priest—planned the Mass and the magnificent music. Twelve of his colleagues—all in white vestments—walked in procession down the aisle with the casket and joined him on the altar. It looked like a convention of angels! As a matter of fact, they sang a High Mass that is called the Mass of the Angels.

I kept thinking of a sampler she had embroidered and framed in her kitchen. It said: "Make it do. Wear it out. Use it up. Do without." That's the way she lived. But she was buried with ceremony that would do justice to a cardinal. I was happy she left with such style.

She did one wild thing a few months before she died. One of our friends has an annual Christmas party, and Anne went to Marshall Field's designer room and bought herself a dress for $1,200! I keep remembering her dancing the cha-cha in that beautiful black-net cocktail dress. I will hold that picture in my mind forever.

A week after the funeral, an invitation came into the office to sail on a new ship out of Athens. I decided to go. I don't know why I kid myself that changing my geography changes my life—because it never does. You take yourself with you. (I have a friend who says, "Wherever I go, the son-of-a-bitch is there!")

The last time I was on a ship in the Greek islands, I was

with my husband, Julie. It brings back nice memories to be here, but it also reminds me that I am still alone.

I'm lonely. It's been over a year. I always heard it only took a year to recover. What's wrong with me?

That's all for now. Will write from Chicago. I hope I find a letter from you when I get home.

Love,
Corinne

Mr. John Hibbler
John Hibbler Interiors
875 Michigan Avenue
Chicago, IL 60611

Dear John—

Enclosed is my check for the lamp you ordered. It came yesterday and it looks so nice next to the white chair—just as you predicted.

I so appreciate all your wonderful help in redecorating the house. The lighter color in the living room brightens up everything, and I love my new drapes.

You were so right when you said it would give me a lift to have everything so fresh and clean!

Thanks for being such a good decorator and loyal friend!

Love,
Corinne

Lonely

lonely

no excuse for it

lonely

"some people just don't know how to occupy themselves"
everyone knows that

lonely

"an intelligent person is never bored"
everyone knows that

lonely

sitting alone
in a perfect room
the new lamp has arrived
the decorator says
it warms that corner

lonely

sitting alone
in a perfect house
the cleaning service
has polished
the already clean

lonely

there's a movie I want to see
I don't go

lonely

Can I speak to Julius Edwards, please?

Julius is not here. Who is this?

This is the Clinique cosmetic counter at Bloomingdales, and we wanted to tell Julius about a special offer we have.

Julius doesn't wear Clinique cosmetics.

Oh, I'm sorry. According to our records he has been a Clinique customer in the past.

I don't think so. Maybe it's because the charge account is still in his name.

Well, will you tell Julius we called? And tell him that we have a special going on?

When I see him, I'll tell him.

Thank you very much.

Dear Sheila,

Where are you? I'm starting to become alarmed. No word for months. Thought I'd write anyway to let you know what is happening. I need your advice. I don't know who else I can ask. You are too far away to have me locked up.

Julie is still in this house. He even talks to me, Sheila.

The other morning, for example, I was really in a sweat, doing my aerobics. You know how you get when you're really overextending your capacity. It's like you go into some altered state of consciousness.

I've been reading a lot of books on investing. You know how Julie was. He never talked about his business. If I'd ask what the market did today, he'd tell me, "Read the paper." Anyway, I have to find out what to do with money, so I've been studying.

Back to the story. While I was doing my aerobics, I heard Julie's voice in my head—so clearly—that said, "If you want to play, put a buy order in for IBM at 120. It will probably go through that to 118, but don't be a pig. As soon as you get it, put a sell in at 130. You'll pick up a little fast, safe money." I swear to God this happened.

Wait. There's more. This is the startling part. He then added, "Buy five hundred shares of Standard Oil of Indiana at the market. Hold it. I'll let you know when to sell."

I looked in the paper. IBM was at 152. I could not find Standard Oil of Indiana anywhere.

I called my broker. I am doing business with this gal Alice. She worked with Julie for thirty years. As a matter of fact, when I used to ask him who to use, in the unlikely event he would not be here, he would tell me, "No one. They will all churn your money." After he died, I remembered Alice. He always disapproved of women in business, but he used to begrudgingly admit that Alice was pretty smart.

I told Alice the story and that I could not find Standard Oil of Indiana in the paper. She laughed (kind of) and said all the older brokers still refer to Amoco by its old name. She also said that if anyone could communicate from the grave it would be Julie.

I bought Amoco. She put in the order for IBM, rather reluctantly. The rest is history. IBM did hit 118. I did sell at 130. I made over $5,000!

Sheila, what do you make of all this? I remember that you mentioned that after your son died, you used to feel him around you. Am I crazy or what?

Funny, it does not scare me at all. As a matter of fact, it is kind of nice to have him around taking care of me.

You know, now that I think about it, I had such a strange feeling when I went to buy the flowers for the yard this spring. I kept putting things back as though someone did not approve the choice. Like someone else was in charge. You remember what an avid gardener he was.

Please advise me with every thought you have about the above.

Love,
Corinne

Dear Junie Bug,

I can't believe that you actually went along with Doug's plan
to go CAMPING with the whole family in the Adirondacks for
THREE WEEKS! You are really a good sport. I hope the mos-
quitoes don't make a complete mess of you.

I am thankful you left me a post office box number at
camp headquarters. I guess you nuts have to come in to take
a shower sometime. Give me a luxury hotel with a marble
bath every time.

Things are the same around here. Except maybe, just
maybe, I am starting to come alive by thinking I should get
out a little bit with the possibility of meeting someone (read
that "a man").

Don't laugh, but I thought I'd start by shaping up my lingerie wardrobe. Everything I own would qualify me to be a
Girl Scout leader. The good old cotton club. And I read this
article in *Cosmopolitan* that said you should wear sexy
underwear to feel "secretly seductive."

So, two weeks ago, I went to Neiman Marcus and bought
a ton—don't even ask what I spent—of transparent, extravagant, decadent underwear—including a flaming red teddy!
I completely lost my mind.

Well, it has not worked. I'm returning everything that I
haven't worn. Not one living soul noticed anything different
about me. Nobody seemed to know I was now secretly
seductive.

I now know the real problem. No one noticed because I
need to lose five to ten pounds. All this fat is getting in the

way of my secret. Then I will go back and buy everything again in a smaller size. Just to show you how serious I am, I have joined a health club and I am going to exercise EVERY DAY!

So that brings us up to date. I didn't want you to miss any news while you were out of civilization.

Try your best to have a good time in that godforsaken place and call me as soon as you walk in the door at home.

Love you—

Your soon-to-be skinny and sexy sister,
Corinne

SEPTEMBER

HOLIDAYS THIS MONTH
Labor Day—4th
First Day of Rosh Hashanah—25th

QUOTE FOR THIS MONTH
"Change starts when someone sees
the next step."
—WILLIAM DRAYTON

THINGS TO DO THIS MONTH

lose weight!
Go to the club
EVERY DAY!

SUN	MON	TUE	WED	THUR	FRI	SAT
				1 7 AM EastBank Club	**2** 7 AM East Bank Club	
3 7AM East Bank Club	**4** 7 AM East Bank Club	**5** 7 AM East Bank Club	**6** 7 AM East Bank Club	**7** 7 A EBC	**8** 7 A EBC	**9** 7 A EBC
10	**11** 7 A EBC	**12**	**13**	**14** 7 A EBC	**15**	**16**
17	**18**	**19**	**20** 7 AM EBC	**21**	**22**	**23**
24	**25**	**26**	**27**	**28** 7 A EBC	**29**	**30**

Dearest Julie—

It seems a little strange to be writing to a dead person, but since you seem to be around, maybe there is some kind of post office that can deliver a letter to you.

First of all, I want to thank you for all the years we spent together. If there is such a thing as a grade for marriages, I think we would get a solid A for effort. Most of the years were wonderful, and although we didn't always agree (maybe even most of the time), we sure learned a lot about love and forgiveness. Finally, I think we came to a real peace in our relationship. And the tenderness and care you received from our sons at the sad end of your life is a testimonial that we must have done something right together.

But now I have to move on. It has been nice to have you watching over the household as usual, but you see, sometime in the future I will want a real live person in my life. I will never get that if you are constantly here telling me what to do.

I wrote you a little poem explaining my feelings. Please do not take this as rejection. I don't mean it that way. I am being practical, which is something you always claimed I never was.

It is time for me to take over my own life. I know you probably don't think I can do that alone, but you have to let me try.

Please know that I wish you all the peace and joy you deserve. Thanks for all the beautiful memories. You will always have a special place in my heart.

With love forever,
Corinne

Time to Go

You can't stay here anymore,
sleep on your side of the bed,
watch TV at your end of the couch,
tell me what stocks to buy,
oppose your son's change of major,
or pick out flowers for the yard.

This is my house now.
I like the color I painted the living room,
and I always hated those drapes.
THAT CHAIR DOES SO NEED REUPHOLSTERING!

I accept all your apologies:
that you didn't know how much you loved me,
didn't appreciate me until you died,
didn't leave enough insurance,
never meant to make me cry.
I forgive you.

I KNOW YOU'RE PROUD OF ME!
YOU'VE TOLD ME A MILLION TIMES!

Please. Go away now.

I have taken down your father's picture
and, I'm sorry,
all of yours,
put away my wedding ring,
picked up the pieces of my heart.

I'm waiting for a new life to start,

and you can't stay here anymore.

Getting Out

Dear Sheila,

Finally, I hear from you! Why in the world did they send you to live on a rubber plantation? I thought you were going to develop a radio station and little theater groups!

What a story about the old wife thinking she had to share her toothless husband with you! Turning her down must have been a stretch of even your diplomacy. I hope you are thinking of writing a book about all this.

Thanks for your thoughts on my ghost. As it turned out, I did what you said to do.

I heard about a psychic named Robert and went to see him. He told me Julie was not going on to "the light," wherever that is, and that I was the one holding him here. We did a process of cutting the cord between us and guess what? Julie is not here anymore. Of course I now have another problem. Shall I hold Amoco or sell?

I have lost my broker. Alice really freaked out when IBM hit 118. She does not return my calls.

I'm glad you like the poems. From this new batch you can tell that I am feeling better. But what a strange thing to be dating again at my age. I get so nervous. I feel like a teenager.

I put an ad in the lonely hearts column. Yes, you heard me right. Don't worry. It is perfectly safe. They answer to a box number and have no idea who I am. Some of the replies are priceless.

But at least some of my friends are more satisfied that I am getting out. There is so much pressure to have a man in your life.

Glad you are where you can take a shower. Nice to have my pen pal back.

Love,
Corinne

P.S. I am thinking of having my eyes lifted—will let you know if I decide to do it.

Getting Out

They told me I should get out more,
see new people.
I'd never meet anyone
sitting in the house.
So I thought
I'd try it—
but I'll go alone.
In case I hate it,
I can just go home.

I bought a ticket
to a Beethoven concert.
The music was beautiful
and I realized I had to quit smoking,
not for health reasons.
Standing alone at intermission
having a cigarette
is terrifying.
So I just went home.

Signed up for a class in tarot.
Each student at the table
had a crystal (don't touch it!)
as big as a fist.

The instructor had three.
Before I found a crystal
that spoke to me,
I just went home.

There was the Over-Forty Singles Club.
An elderly man asked me to dance,
which surprised me.
I saw him come in.
He could hardly walk.
He was concealing an erection
that would have shamed a twenty-year-old.
I just went home.

I went to a town board meeting.
There was a motion on the floor
to buy the police department a coffeepot.
After it was seconded and passed,
they argued for an hour.
Before I bought the cops a pot,
I just went home.

At the Consciousness Raising Center,
a good place to meet interesting people,
I was assigned to a group
to explore protections from spirit entity invaders.
I didn't know they were out,

and before one of them invaded me,
I just went home.

Visited a widows support group.
They cried a lot.
The lecture for the evening was on how to write a check,
and the mystery of the bank statement.
Before I started to feel too superior,
I just went home.

At the Council on Foreign Relations,
a fat banker from Citicorp
mesmerized the audience with information
on a South American monetary crisis.
Before I announced it had been in all the papers,
I just went home.

I have not found my niche yet.

Lonely Hearts Ad

One lady who never thinks of herself as middle-aged
and still looks at thirty-year-olds as possibilities
until she remembers,
with stretch marks,
street smarts,
vaginal dryness
but very nice eyes,
who is starting her diet and aerobics on Monday
and is saving for an eyelift,
not quite emotionally secure
nor, if the truth be known, financially
(plays the market),
devours self-improvement books
and hasn't improved,
with a touch of arthritis,
a slightly elevated cholesterol,
but who has recently discovered a Higher Power,

Looking for

a mature Tom Cruise type, tanned, fit, spiritual,
romantic, terrific dancer, rich as Croesus, kind as Jesus,
totally devoted, into worshiping, hates eating
at home, is sexually eager, brilliant, flies first class,
adores shopping, caviar, and suites on world cruises.

Dearest Peter—

Thanks for your nice letter. Although it is wonderful to talk on the phone, I always appreciate it when you make the time to write.

What great news that MGM is taking one of your songs for a movie. I can't wait to hear you in a theater near me!

Dad always worried about your choosing a profession that is so associated with the drug culture. So it was nice to hear that club managers screen musicians carefully for drug usage. Not because they are judgmental but because they are running a business and want the group to show up and play!

I know your head is on straight in this area, but I do worry about some of the people you meet. It gave this mother pause when you were home for Christmas and I overheard you telling your friends stories of groupies who rush the dressing room after the show in raincoats—with nothing else underneath!

But I trust you, Peter. I know under that long hair is an intelligent, beautiful, and sensitive human being with good standards. And I know you read about diseases like everyone else. But please be careful. You are precious cargo for me and the family.

Excuse me for worrying and the lecturing, but that's what mothers are supposed to do. It's our job.

Everything is coming along fine around here. Alex and I are so looking forward to seeing you when we come to Los Angeles over his spring break. It will be a thrill for us to see your name on the marquee at the Lingerie Club. What does one wear to those clubs? I want to bring the right clothes so I don't disgrace you!

We are also anxious to meet Paul's new girlfriend. You are going to have to explain your comment "I like Linda. It's just that after about fifteen minutes of her, I have to leave. She makes my eye twitch!"

I love you and I so admire your creative talents!

Mom

P.S. Your new day job as a receptionist in a law firm sounds interesting—they accepted your long hair because they specialize in discrimination cases! This could only happen in Los Angeles. Do you think you could ever get interested in law?

Dear Bill,

It was very generous of you to write and explain why you will not be seeing me again. It is important for a woman who is reentering the human race to know the reasons she flunked out on her first date.

I feel very bad that you had to go to the emergency room for treatment of your asthma right after you left me. I had no idea you were allergic to smoke.

I would not hurt a nice man like you for anything. I do hope you will recover from the ordeal quickly.

Thank you for the nice dinner. You have such lovely table manners.

Cordially, and with apologies,
Corinne Edwards

P.S. Have you thought about taking an assertiveness training course?

Middle-Age Dating

Wait a minute!

I'm not up on the rules
and I need to know—

The man buys two dinners—
and after the third,
I'm the dessert—
right?

Wait a minute!

I like you.
And it's lonely
with only Stouffers
plus the six o'clock news.
And some striking similarities
have surfaced.
We both play the market,
like Puerto Vallarta,

and it's not even that I'm stingy
about sharing my body,
but is that a firm enough foundation

that I can view your bare belly
and feel abandon?
Is there sex past sag?

I'm willing to pay for my own dinner,
no, wait a minute,
pay for your dinner,

if you'll give me a chance
to get used to the rules.

Dearest Junie Bug—

In case you think you're missing something by being married, I'm going to tell you about my latest date.

We met for lunch. He is a friend of a friend of a client of mine. As we settled in, I, half-joking, asked him, "Well, here we are. Why don't you tell me the story of your life?"

He started from where he was born in Iowa—no, wait a minute, to how his parents met, that's an interesting story. He was a late walker. Didn't talk until he was three. It was probably an emotional problem. His mother favored his brother, which probably led to the stuttering problem.

But wait, he skipped telling me about his kindergarten teacher. She was beautiful. He was in love with her.

On to the childhood diseases—chickenpox was the worst, unless you want to count the tonsillectomy. He had won an essay contest in the seventh grade, but he hated high school. Those teachers were hard markers.

His first date stood him up. He didn't make the football team.

June, after two hours, the coffee had not arrived and we were only up to age twenty.

It was finally over. And as he left he said, "I can't wait to see you again. I have never met such an interesting conversationalist."

Just to keep you up-to-date. This single life is a jungle out here!

Love you,
Corinne

Hello, Corinne. This is Eric.

Hello, Eric.

I was wondering if we could get together on Friday night.

Oh, I'm sorry, I'm busy on Friday.

What about Saturday or Sunday?

I have plans for the weekend.

Well, when can I see you?

Eric, it was nice being with you last week. But you know, I don't think this is a fit between us.

What do you mean?

I just don't think we have a lot in common.

So you won't see me again?

I think it would be better.

I paid for your dinner, you know.

Yes?

I am not used to being made a jerk out of. I don't just buy dinners for people.

I'll send you a check for my dinner. How much was it?

You damn well better pay for your own dinner. It was $24. I'll send you a copy of the bill.

Don't bother. I'm writing the check out right now. I have your office address.

Look, maybe you'll change your mind. I'll call you in a week.

Don't call. Good-bye, Eric.

Dear Paul and Peter—

I know that Alex must have been the one who tipped you off that I was placing personal ads, not any psychic "little bird" as you claim.

Believe me, I am not taking any chances on going out with a serial killer and no, there is no service that runs checks on the men who answer. You are just going to have to trust me. I was not born yesterday or even the day before, and I will not take any wild chances. I always meet these people in a public place and never give out my home telephone number until I am sure that he is just a nice, normal guy looking for a date.

I also wish you would talk to Alex about his attitude. It has been two years since Dad died, and I really don't need to hear his "I hope I'm not going to have to see that guy at breakfast!" comment after every man he meets. I think you all know that no one will be here at breakfast unless he's a serious contender for my hand!

I know you all love me and are concerned for me, so I am not mad—but please!

I love all you boys,
Mom

Manpower

Who says there are no men out there?

I placed an ad in the lonely hearts column and got forty replies:

- a con man who wanted to sell me mortgages
- an eighty-year-old who said he was fifty
- an oncologist who claimed his wife would love me
- a paper salesman who wanted to wear my clothes
- a psychologist whose wife had died two days ago
- a lawyer who sent me a bill for my dinner
- an author who wanted my replies for his book
- a politician who requested a donation
- a lifer who claimed he was innocent
- a man who claimed he knew me and why hadn't I picked him up at the bus stop
- a retiree who asked me to marry him immediately
- a retiree who said he didn't want to marry me but had graduated from Harvard
- three illegal immigrants needing green cards
- an engineer who negotiated sex over the first cocktail
- a man with twelve children whose wife didn't understand him
- lots of lonely people I still feel guilty about not calling

I'm thinking about running the ad again next week.

Dear Junie Bug,

Greetings from Machu Picchu—the lost city of the Incas! Even I surprise myself at the places I wind up! What an incredible experience to be in this major ruin! I am taking lots of pictures to show you where I've been. The scenery here in the Andes Mountains makes you feel like you are living in a postcard. During the day, we explore. At night, there is absolutely nothing to do so I have time to write.

Thanks for your nice long letter, which I had no time to answer before I left. But I brought it along, so I'll use this quiet time to answer all your questions.

No, I will not be going to cousin Joy's sixth wedding in San Francisco. We got a special offer in the office, and I am taking all the boys to Club Med that week. Then, two weeks later I am leaving for a Black Sea cruise. Anyway, I have credit with Joy. I made the trip to her last wedding. (Tell you what. I'll go to her next wedding! Meow!)

And no, the ad I sent you was not the one I put in the newspaper. That was a joke to amuse myself. You can't tell the truth about yourself and what you want in a lonely hearts ad and expect anyone to answer! I wrote a very conservative ad and the results were amazing. I don't know if it is just our age or that turnover is high at this time, but there are a lot of single men out there. Have met some nice people but not *the one.* I wonder if I ever will.

One thing has become very apparent to me. Men do not adjust as well as women to being alone. For example, I went out a few times with a psychologist who answered my ad. He told me, on our first date, that he was a recent widower. Three months later, he mentioned that his wife died on October 30. The letter he wrote in answer to my ad was dated November 1! He must have written to me from the funeral home!

I am so happy that Allison was accepted at her first-choice college. Just think. After all these years, you'll be able to think about Junie instead of all those kids. At first I felt lonely when Alex got his own apartment. Now, although I love to have him drop over or stay overnight (he finds it difficult to separate himself from his Mommy and her washer and dryer), I don't feel so bad when he leaves. It's wonderful to have the boys come home for holidays and visits, but then it's nice to have my peaceful (read that "neat") house back when they leave.

Now I am going to tell you a secret. I went to see a plastic surgeon, and I am going to have my eyes done! Don't tell anyone in the family. It will be interesting to see if anyone notices. (At these prices, they better!) I figure why not look as good as you can? My appointment is still two months off so I have lots of time to get up my nerve.

I appreciate your remembering the third anniversary of Julie's death. It feels like it was so long ago and like it all happened to a different person. My life has changed so much since then. I still think about him and miss him. But they told me, "Life goes on." And it is true. It has. Somehow being in this ancient, ghostly ruin makes me realize how fragile and short our time is in this world.

I hope you get this letter. I don't know how they get the mail out of here. Maybe by horse.

When I get home we'll decide on a date for our "Big Apple Experience." In the meantime, much love to everyone. Keep lots of it for yourself.

Your devoted sister,
Corinne

Dearest Alie—

Sorry I won't be home when you arrive to do your wash today but there are cold cuts in the refrigerator for lunch and some beef stew for you to take home for dinner.

One small request.

I know you were trying to help me last week when you came to do your laundry but PLEASE don't include any of my things with yours.

My white bathroom towels are now a beautiful shade of pink. You were probably trying to save soap when you threw them in with your red sweats.

You might also consider separating your colors. I shudder to think what shade your underpants are.

Love you and always appreciate your kind thoughts—

Mom

Transfusion

It was just a fling.
I mean,
how serious can you get with a person
who has read ten books in his entire life
and thought
Johann Sebastian Bach
was a portrait painter?

The scenario:
A successful, older woman.
Him.
Muscles. Fascinated.
Unsuitable.

Who knew he'd be kind—so gentle.
Who expected
he would flood the corners of my mind
with sunshine?
Make me laugh.

It was difficult to give him up.

I saw him today,
and when he told me he missed me

and he'd always be my friend,
I wanted to reach out
and touch his face.
Kiss the corner of his clean mouth.
Feel that hard body against mine.

I had to be very stern with myself.
He had not read one book since I had seen him last.

But after all—
Bach's been dead for years.

Dear Paul—

Peter said that you are working day and night on an important new commercial for your company, so it has been hard to catch you at home. I thought I would drop you a line so you know you still have a family out here.

You have always been the one with the greatest gift for concentration—a kind of tunnel vision. When you are involved in a project, nothing exists outside of it. I remember once, when you were in college and studying for finals, we had to send you a telegram to tell you to pay your phone bill as the service had been turned off for three weeks. You didn't even notice that no one had called!

Sometimes I wonder how you three boys could come from the same genes and the same environment and be so different. You, so serious and intense—Peter, the party, people person—and Alex, so straightlaced and conservative. It has been interesting to be the mother of this group—a real exercise for me in accepting people just as they are.

But aside from these differences, there is a powerful union—a strong bond of loyalty and love. Peter framed it perfectly when he once said, "Only one of us has to make it. We'll take the others along with us." I keep that thought in mind when I see you arguing and baiting each other!

Sorry about the breakup with Linda. I hope you are not feeling too bad about it. She seemed like a nice person and was certainly beautiful and glamorous! These aspiring actresses sure seem to have it all. I hope you have gotten over being mad at Alex for saying, "What's the difference?

She looks like the last girlfriend he broke up with. Blond. Blue-eyed and boobs." You know how conservative he is (maybe he's jealous).

What I'm waiting for is a girl who looks like Linda who can cook and wants to stay home and give you babies!

Okay, I've said it. You just have to put up with me.

Remember, I love you, Paul. Good luck with the commercial. Call when you realize there are phones in the house.

Mom

Dear Gail,

Thanks for the brochure on the seminar "Solving Past Lives in Your Present." I've been going to a lot of self-improvement workshops, but I don't think I am interested in attending one on this subject.

My present is so complicated and cluttered with stuff going on now. I couldn't possibly drag anything from another life into it.

Hope you have a good time. Take notes.

Love you,
Corinne

Consciousness Woo Woo Circuit

My cousin Gail has a heavy schedule.

Monday she goes for rebirthing,
Tuesday to her Chinese wholistic doctor
(I gave her my corn pot to boil the herbs),
Wednesday for Bodywork,
Thursday to Overeaters Anonymous,
Friday for *A Course in Miracles*.
Saturday, she's busiest of all—
smudging at the Earth Wisdom meeting
followed by her tai chi lesson,
ending with a hypnotherapy session.

In between,
she practices out-of-body experiences,
does crystal meditations
(her crystal is charged with finding a lover
and curing her candida),
studies neurolinguistics,
channels her spirit guide,
and is focused on unconditional love.

She has quit her job
because it interferes with her abundance.

Every Sunday morning
she calls to tell me how miserable she is.
Her friends all live in the present
and she can't get a straight answer from anyone.

Don't suggest:
Past life regression, graphology, palmistry, transcendental
    meditation, tarot, numerology, firewalking, Arnold
    Patent, Wicca, *I Ching,* Reiki, sweat lodges, bioener-
    getics, aromatic therapy—
that phone psychic in Texas
who has access to the Akashic records—
The Forum, or, God forbid, astrology.
(She has a Saturn return and won't discuss it!)
She's done all that.

I guess it's better
than just hanging around
waiting for things to improve . . .

Dr. Thomas Picardy—Plastic Surgeon
1500 North Lake Shore Drive
Chicago, IL 60618

Dear Dr. Picardy:

I want to thank you for the wonderful job you did at lifting my eyelids and eliminating the bags under them.

I just have a tiny bit of criticism.

I think you should make it very clear to your people who are having this done that this procedure requires cutting. Further, it should be explained how terrible they will look immediately afterward.

I know you gave me material to read and even suggested that I take ten days off from work, but you see, I did not believe you. I guess what I am trying to say is that you are a very fine doctor who should work on being more BELIEV-ABLE. Perhaps there is some kind of course for doctors who suffer from this difficulty.

To help you, I am enclosing an article I wrote, based on my experience, which I am submitting to *Plastic Surgeons Monthly*. Naturally, I will not use your name.

You have my permission to duplicate it and pass it out to your patients while you are working on your problem. I think it is important for people to know what really happens.

Again, thank you for making me look so nice.

Sincerely,
Corinne Edwards

Eyelift Diary

Wednesday Afternoon

I must admit, I feel a little nervous. It's like you feel when you're going to a new beauty shop—it's the same thing. You know how it is. You don't know if this new stylist is scissors happy and will completely ruin your hair, or get the color all wrong, or what. I remember the time that manicurist cut my cuticle and got it all infected. So sure, I have a few apprehensions. I still can't figure out why that doctor made me come in here so early. I left my desk a mess.

They are so serious in this hospital. I told them, look, I am just having my eyes lifted. Not a big deal. I don't need all this blood work, X rays, and that heart test. I said, this is ridiculous. You'd think I was having a liver transplant or something. And another thing that is strange. Everything has to be paid up front. Even the doctor. Can you imagine? You'd think I was going to die or something and not pay the bill.

Anyway, I am just going to calm down and not let them aggravate me. Tomorrow, it will all be over and that will be that. It will be great not to have my eyeshadow clumping on my eyelids anymore, and let's face it, Erase is no longer doing anything for the bags under my eyes.

Like I was telling my sister, after forty it is patch-patch-

patch. When you get older, you have to take care of yourself or you fall apart. You should go to the health club every morning and once in a while take two days off and have your eyes done.

Well, at least I got the private room I requested. That was touch and go. And the phone is on. Good. My office must think I died. I told them I'd call in two hours ago. They will never believe all the tests I had to go through for a simple procedure.

Wednesday Night

My girlfriend Ruthie had just arrived with the snacks and a thermos of coffee to celebrate, when this strange foreign doctor came in. I explained to him that I had my own doctor and that my doctor had all the information he needed on me, but this new doctor would not go away. He could hardly speak English but he wanted to know when I first noticed my condition. I could not believe it. And interrupting us like that. He saw I had company. Anyway, I told him my eyes started falling right after I was born and it continued until now. He had no sense of humor at all. Finally he left. I told Ruth, "What is all this fuss about?" I hope I can sleep in this bed. It is terrible.

Thursday Morning

These nurses really throw their weight around. I did not sleep a wink with all the racket they made all night. One came and had a fit because I was smoking. Then, she really screamed at me because I asked her to call down and rush my breakfast. You won't believe this, but at these prices they do not even include breakfast! She wouldn't even get me a cup of coffee. It is a disgrace the way they run this place.

Just then the anesthesiologist came in. Another foreign doctor, but at least she spoke English. I thought she'd be a little more understanding. I told her, "Look, I am not into pain. I do not want to feel anything. I mean, *out* is where I want to be, for the whole thing." She said I was not having a general anesthetic, which I do not remember being informed about. It was not necessary and could be dangerous—I could stop breathing. So I said, "Wait a minute. I have canceled my appointments for the entire day and don't have to breathe that much. Just take care of it and I won't bother you again." It's ridiculous how you have to tell these people their own business.

The guy who came in with the stretcher was very rude. I tried to explain to him that I was talking on the phone to one of my most important clients about a trip to London. My client's wife is claustrophobic and has asthma and it was very important to get them seats on British Airways as far forward as possible in the nonsmoking section. He wouldn't listen. I said, "Look, this is business. First things first."

Well, as it turned out, it was just as well he interrupted me because I started feeling a little funny about then.

Probably from that shot they gave me. I hope I didn't get the wrong seats. I'll have to recheck it when I get back to the room.

On the way downstairs, I noticed that the walls could really use a coat of paint and I made a mental note to mention it to my doctor. He's on the board here. Somebody has to report these things—Oh! Here he is. Boy, green is definitely not his color. He should have his colors done. It changes your life.

It
makes a difference   they   don't push   I
can move   over   myself

Thursday Afternoon

cry ing
     can't stop crying
what time is it?   take
these off   can't see   better no   I can
walk   myself to the   bathroom   leave me
     alone
mirror   who   is   that?
what have they   done?
bloody stitches   swollen   hurts   help
     weak
Why didn't anybody tell me this was an operation????

104

Friday

I know I told the office I would be in today but I would not even put my hand outside the door to reach for the mail. Let me tell you, I am a mess. I hope they got the license of that truck that hit me. Anyway, as soon as I got home, I had my lawyer on the phone right away. He had the nerve to tell me to read what I signed. Give me a break. I have enough to read for my business as it is.

I now know that I made a colossal mistake. I mean, I sent this client down to the Cayman Islands and she had her entire face done and her belly tucked and she said it was a nothing. And, when I tell you, cheap! It was a regular vacation. The salt water down there heals everything in one day.

I don't know when I'll be able to go back to work. The way I look, I told them in about a year.

Two Weeks Later

Didn't I tell you? I thought I told you I was going to have my eyes fixed. Believe me, it is just a small procedure. A piece of cake. You ought to think about having it done. But, wait, only use my doctor. I am telling you, he is terrific. Now, he's not cheap. But I always say, go to Loehmann's for your clothes but not your face! Definitely do it. It's a lot of fun. Ruthie and I will come over to see you in the hospital and bring some snacks. But I mean, do it! It's a NOTHING!

Dear Paul and Peter—

Alex tells me you were a little perturbed that I didn't tell you the exact day when I was having the little operation on the bags over and under my eyes.

I decided to wait and tell you when it was over because I know that you three worry about the slightest thing.

Anyway, it is all over and I can't wait for you to see the new me! Although people who see me don't know exactly what is different, it is a great improvement. I get comments like "You look so good today" and "Did you just get back from a vacation? You look so rested."

I'll see you in three weeks when we meet at Club Med and you'll tell me that I definitely did the right thing. People are going to think I am your sister!

Look, if it had been something serious, you would have been told.

Love from your twenty-year-old—
Mom

Dear Molly,

I cannot tell you how sad I am about the recent passing of your beloved Harry. I know how devastated you must be. I remember what it was like to go through such a loss.

His funeral was so beautiful. Your minister spoke eloquently about the beautiful marriage the two of you enjoyed for thirty years.

I hope, through your sobs, that you were able to take solace in his eulogy.

I am looking forward to being with you soon. We single gals have to support each other.

Please know that I am feeling your pain and grieving with you.

Much love,
Corinne

Merry Widow

My girlfriend Molly, a recent widow,
confessed to me
that her new single status is not as bad
as she thought it would be.

She . . .

- no longer has to hide new clothes
- can keep the light on and finish the book
- eats cornflakes for dinner at 10 P.M.
- buys art without approval
- painted the front door red
- comes home anytime she wants
- doesn't have to justify redecorating
- never has to watch *The Today Show* again
- is trading the sedan in for a convertible
- has ordered a silly license plate
- can have weird friends
- is paying $200 for a psychic reading
- doesn't have to listen to complaints about the market
- has a kitchen countertop without a briefcase on it
- gives the kids money when they need it
- is looking at condos on Lake Shore Drive
- has fired his lawyer, who is a stuffed shirt

- has changed banks
- is finally testing out her vaginal repair job

So—she added, confidentially—

Other than not having an escort
who never wanted to go anywhere anyway,
life is not half bad.

But, don't tell anyone.
She's grieving.

Dear Paul and Peter—

Thanks for your nice letter thanking me for the wonderful trip to Club Med. We sure had a lot of fun!

Obviously, you two and your brother Alex had some private talks about my conduct with that Maurice fellow I met there.

The fact that he never paid me back for his sightseeing excursions and that he smoked only my cigarettes for the entire week does not mean that I am looking for a gigolo boyfriend. Although he is a nice person, do you really think I would consider a long-term relationship with a man who writes porno copy for a sexual aids catalog? I think not.

But I will tell you this: Anyone who can dance as well as Maurice is worth a few dollars and cigarettes. But you don't have to worry that he is your next father.

Sometimes I wonder if you think I am your daughter or your mother?

Love you all anyway!

Mom

Dear kids at the office—

The Black Sea is something we should concentrate on selling. This is a fabulous trip. Imagine sitting at the table in Yalta where Stalin and Roosevelt and Churchill signed that epic agreement!

I am having a lot of fun. The captain has a crush on me. I do have to add, however, that I have a rival. He has a meaningful relationship with vodka! I don't know who drives this ship at night. Certainly not him. Fascinates me how all his officers cover up for him. A textbook codependency scenario going on here! Every morning, I see him on the deck and he asks, "Was everything all right last night?" He does not know if we are having an affair or not. In the meantime, I'm getting a lot of deferential treatment on board as the captain's sweetheart. (No! Of course I'm not!)

I know you haven't seen much of me lately but I do still work there!

Love to all,
Corinne

Dear Dave,

It was nice to see you again while you were attending your convention in Chicago. You are looking well.

However, I was surprised that there were three calls from you on my voice mail when I returned home today.

I thought I should recap our final conversation so there is no misunderstanding: I KNOW THAT YOUR WIFE IS AWAY FOR THREE FULL WEEKS BUT THAT IS NOT LONG ENOUGH FOR ME.

I hope her mother is feeling better.

Best regards,
Corinne

Married . . . But

It's so lovely to be involved with a married man.
He can see you between 8 A.M. and 6 P.M., weekdays,
on alternate Tuesday nights,
his night out with the boys,
and any time his wife visits her mother in Texas.

It's broadening to travel with a married man.
He knows this fabulous restaurant in Akron,
there are cultural things in Wichita
you never imagined,
and if you can fly out on Wednesday
he'll get you a ticket,
but he's not free until after his six o'clock meeting,
and of course you know
not to pick up the phone in the room.

It's so comforting to see a married man.
He's never around when you have the flu,
your face erupts,
your back goes out,
you're overdrawn,
or in the morning
when the mascara smudges under your eyes,
on your birthday, Christmas, New Year's, and
the Fourth of July.

It's so sexy to be with a married man.
He's so eager,
not having slept with his wife for ten years now,
being misunderstood, deprived and all,
he knows positions you've only read about,
and he'll do anything to save you
from being a sex-starved fossil,
from herpes, and god forbid, AIDS,
and even promiscuity,

although he wouldn't stand in your way
if the right guy came along,
but dammit, that man would have to pass muster,
the whole thing being silly talk anyway
because of his knowing you were meant to be together
as soon as his wife's mother dies
(he owes her that),
the last kid graduates college,
and his lawyer transfers things—

Oh, it's so lovely.

Dear Junie Bug—

Thanks so much for your nice long letter. I am sorry you are having such a difficult time since Allison went off to college.

I am sure that you will get used to being alone eventually. After all, Doug does come home every weekend. It's not as though you have no company at all.

It does seem that the precautions you are taking for your safety are slightly excessive. You always used to say that the last crime in your neighborhood was fifty years ago when someone stole a chicken.

I will try to tape Snoopy barking at the mail carrier. How many barks do you think you need? There is a slight problem because we have a new mail carrier and Snoopy likes her so far. But I will do my best for you.

Sorry this is such a short letter. I will write more soon.

Love from your devoted sister,
Corinne

Alone at Last

The last of her six children has left—
and my sister June,
who had dreamed of this day
when she'd loll about in an immaculate house
eating chocolate-chocolate-chip ice cream
which had survived in her freezer for an entire week,
reading novels, refinishing furniture,
listening to Chopin, doing her nails,
having friends over for dessert,
and never, ever, cooking a meal again,
is hysterical.

Her husband travels—
she has placed a stuffed German shepherd in
her front window,
installed view-ruining drapes,
automatic light timers,
and despite a life-sized dummy with a hat on
sitting in her living room,
she's afraid to come home after dark.

She is advertising for a boarder—
but in the meantime,
begs for a tape recording of my dog
barking at the mail carrier.

Funny how we didn't know
that when we were dirt poor, most harried,
exhausted and aggravated with all those kids—

it was the happiest time.

Dear Sheila,

I know how disappointed you are that your assignment in Malaysia is coming to an end. It doesn't help to remember that it lasted several years more than you expected. I wish there was something I could say to console you, but there isn't. Each loss we have seems to trigger all the others. They build on each other.

You have made such wonderful friends there. I am sure a lot of people are desolate because you are leaving. You are so loved by the children who have learned a whole new world through you. I hope, at least, they will not keep you waiting too long to know your new assignment. Good-byes are so painful, especially if they are prolonged. I will be anxious to hear about your new adventure.

Here, I am taking a hard look at my adventure that comes under the heading "A Good Man Is Hard to Find." And do you know what? I'm sick of it. I am ready to quit. If there is someone out there, why isn't he looking for me?

All this effort—having my eyes fixed—placing ads—all these strangers I'm dating—running around the world alone—FOR WHAT? What am I trying to prove? I'll tell you, I don't know. I'm tired of the merry-go-round. It is starting to seem pointless.

I'm going to take part of that back. What is pointless are the REASONS I've been doing all these things. Everything comes from my obsession that I have to replace my husband.

My son Paul put my eyelift in perspective for me. When I

told him about it, he said, "Mom, you've gone through a rough time and it shows on your face. You're a beautiful woman. Fix it."

There's nothing wrong with plastic surgery or travel or dating if you've got your head on straight and you do it for yourself and to have fun and to meet some nice people.

Maybe I'm just in a bad mood along with you.

Let me know your news as soon as you know.

Love,
Corinne

Reader Matches
(Women Seeking Men)

Dear Sir or Madam—

Please cancel the second week of the ad I placed in your personals column.

I know that pulling this ad will entail some inconvenience for you so I thought I'd tell you why.

What I said about wanting someone who likes "ethnic restaurants, walks by the lake, fireplaces, travel, commitment, emotional and financial stability, marriage, etc." is just not the real story.

What I really want is a smart, sweet, silly, sexy guy for purposes of mutual adoration, who will pay 50 percent of the expenses around here, unless he doesn't have it, and will pay my half (lovingly) if I don't have it.

When I figure out how to say that, I'll get back to you. Sorry for your trouble.

Corinne Edwards

Mr. A. B. Boarder
Prestige Brokers, Inc.
100 East 42 Street
New York, NY 10019

Dear Mr. Boarder:

I am responding to your advertisement in *Travel Monthly* in which you offer free appraisals to travel agencies who are considering selling.

Edwards Travel Advisors, Inc., has been in business, at the same location, for twenty years. We gross approximately 2.5 million a year with a mix of 90 percent vacation, 10 percent commercial. Our vacation business is high yield because it is mostly international and cruises.

Although I have not made a definite decision to sell, it would be interesting to have your confidential evaluation of what it is worth on the market.

I'm looking forward to hearing from you.

Sincerely,
Corinne Edwards
President

Dear Sheila,

KOREA! What an interesting place to be assigned! Thanks for the postcard letting me know where you are.

Your address is now a USO box number. Are you still with the peace corps? Anyway, I know you will enjoy whatever you are doing. I can't wait to hear all your new experiences.

The news at this end is that I am changing, Sheila. A new person is coming out I hardly know. I am questioning my whole life and all my motivations. What kind of an existence do I have if I don't know who I am? What am I competing for? Who am I trying to please? I have to find out.

I told three men this week that I will not be seeing them anymore. Not because they aren't nice people. But the person they thought they liked was not me. I have put on a mask for so long that I don't know who's there. Not anyone real. Why was I playing that game? So I can say that I'm dating? So someone can buy me dinner? I can afford to buy my own dinner.

Men are being qualified at every turn too. I was talking with a few women the other night and I could not believe our conversation! Every once in a while, I would interrupt and ask, "Do you know we are speaking of human beings?" We did not agree that men are human. And yet, I have seen my boys' hearts broken many times. Men hurt too.

You can imagine what some of my friends are saying. Arlene is in a state of shock that I have gotten rid of three perfectly serviceable men. But I need some time off. I need to be alone, to live empty for a while. I have to work on turning into myself.

I've joined a study group on a spiritual thought system called *A Course in Miracles.* The quote from that book which really got to me was

> Nothing outside yourself can save you.
> Nothing outside yourself can bring you peace.

That's what I have been doing my whole life. Looking outside myself for safety—in business, in relationships, in the world. And nothing has ever made me feel safe. Nothing has worked for very long.

I'm wondering if I have ever been in love. Maybe I looked for men who told me I was lovable so I could love myself. Can I start over at my age? Is it too late? I'm going to find out. I don't have one date in my future. If I ever am involved with a man again, I hope I will have discovered the real me—whoever that may be.

Thanks for listening. Write as soon as you get settled.

Love you,
Corinne

Experts

I had dinner last night
with three women,
all experts at dissecting a species,
not quite human,
called men.

Lawyers, we said,
they're the worst.
Run you down. Read you like a brief.
Just want to win the case.

Doctors.
Cheap.
Completely void of feelings.
No wonder. Those patients die.

Blue collar. Professors.
Too poor.
Real estate, salesmen of any kind.
No stable salary.
Who wants to support these guys?

The corporate variety. All the same.
Put them in a bottle. Shake them up.
You pour out clones. Dull.

Workaholics of any persuasion.
Money but no time.
Terrible in bed.

We all agreed on one thing.
We were looking for a man.

someone not intimidated by our success
someone deep
someone who can communicate
someone perfect

No human types need apply.

E-mail:

Dear Peter—

All these news flashes in one day are overwhelming!
   You got promoted to office manager!
   And—YOU CUT YOUR HAIR????????? (Paul says like a regular person.)
   CONGRATULATIONS, PETER, ON BOTH EVENTS!
   SEND YOUR MOTHER A PICTURE SO I WILL RECOGNIZE YOU WHEN I SEE YOU!

LOVE ALWAYS!
MOM

Dear God, or All That Is, or Infinite Intelligence, Whoever You are up there and I am hoping You are up there—

I need a miracle.

I want a new and more wonderful perception of my life. I ask You for healing. For me, my family, and all those whom I regard as my family. Heal our minds and our hearts.

If it is in keeping with your plans, please send me a man I can love. Arrange for him to love me. Guide us together. I don't want to be alone anymore.

Please lead me and give me wisdom to follow Your directions. And I need vision and simplicity—and courage to accept what I cannot change.

God! Are You out there? Don't be mad at me.

I need a new and more wonderful perception of my whole life.

I need a miracle now!

Corinne

You were right, you know, Julie—
when you told me

the bill goes down when you turn off the lights
the interest on Visa is exorbitant
Neiman Marcus expects to be paid
you don't buy stocks from psychic feelings
going away doesn't solve anything
those people are a waste of time
outside faucets need draining
dead flowers need plucking
the kid next door pushes drugs
my staff in the office are hypochondriacs
jogging is for twenty-year-olds
love in the mouth doesn't count
you don't spend capital
furnaces need service
registering checks prevents overdrafts
family is everything
I'd better grow up
I was lucky to have you
and you didn't ask for much around here

You were right
when you said
I'd appreciate you better
after you had gone.

Magic

Dear Sheila,

What does it mean when you meet a man and see lights all around him?
    Is it my soul mate? You know about these things.

Urgently,
C.

Dearest Junie Bug—

You are not going to believe this! I have met someone!

His name is Joseph and he is handsome, brilliant, sweet, sexy, successful, very, very funny, and guess what? Irish.

Do you remember, years ago, before Mom died, she told me that when she got on the "other side" where she had some real influence, she was going to find and send me an Irish doctor? It's taken her a long time, but this might be him! He's not a medical doctor but he does have a doctorate. You know how she never approved of Julie.

Anyway, on to the story. I met him at that workshop I told you I was attending. On the very last day.

Wait. There's more. Several follow-up support groups have been formed based on the workshop, and I volunteered to have one at my house—and he is in it! I'll get to see him every week. What a setup! We had our first meeting last night.

He seems to be dating a lot but no one in particular. After the meeting, we were all sitting around and he started to talk about his ideal woman.

He said he wanted "someone not too young, trim but busty, reasonably literate, a little crazy but basically a traditional woman who can cook." Hey! That's me!

I keep telling myself, *Don't get excited*. Be friends. But I am excited. He is a doll. Wouldn't it be wonderful if, after all this crazy dating, I have found the ONE?

Keep your fingers crossed.

Your starry-eyed sister—
Corinne

Just Friends

Your date book's overloaded,
your schedule just won't bend,
but if you find a moment,
will you let me be your friend?

Don't tout myself as perfect.
I'm never quite the same.
You'll think you have my number,
then wonder, what's her name?

But I will make you giggle when you're sad,
listen to your woes,
or bake some bread.
I'm not so bad.

My outside's like a magazine,
shiny, smooth, and slick.
I don't expose the centerfold,
the part that makes me tick.

But I will make excuses if you're wrong,
defend your smallest flaw.
We'll work it out
if you belong.

I rarely show I'm frightened,
the little girl inside,
needing you to hug me.
Big girls never cry.

But I will pick you up if you should fall,
anywhere in the universe.
Get to a phone.
I'll take the call.

I never say I'm lonely,
you'll rarely see me bleed,
though I hunger for the touching,
the nurturing I need.

And although I may hint, cajole, scream, seduce, argue,
    persuade, pout, scheme, manipulate, bully, convince,
    agitate, compromise, or negotiate to get my own way,
I have a short attention span.
And I certainly wouldn't let anyone else treat you like
    that.

You don't have to sign a contract
until your earthly end.
But if it's fun from month to month,
will you let me be your friend?

JANUARY

HOLIDAYS THIS MONTH
New Year's Day—1st
Martin Luther King Day—16th

QUOTE FOR THIS MONTH
"Everything starts as somebody's
daydream."
—LARRY NIVEN

THINGS TO DO THIS MONTH

LOSE 5 LBS!
EXCERCISE
EVERY DAY!

SUN	MON	TUE	WED	THUR	FRI	SAT
1 7A.M. East Bank Club	**2** 7 AM. East Bank club	**3** 7A.M East Bank Club	**4** 7A.M East Bank Club	**5** 7A.M. East Bank Club	**6**	**7** 7 AM East Bank club
8	**9**	**10** 7AM East Bank Club	**11**	**12**	**13** 7AM EBC	**14**
15	**16** 7AM EBC	**17**	**18**	**19**	**20**	**21**
22	**23**	**24**	**25** 7AM EBC	**26** 7 AM EBC	**27**	**28**
29	**30**	**31**				

Astrological Computer Service
792 Lampert Drive
Memphis, TN 46524

Dear Sirs:

I am returning the comparative chart you did between me
and a man I have an interest in because I am sure I have the
wrong year.

I cannot tell you exactly the year he was born, and I cannot ask him because I am afraid he'll ask me.

Do you have any kind of a bulk rate for more than one
year of comparison between our charts? I'd like you to do
charts from the year I gave you to five years forward. I am
hoping he is not younger than that.

I am sure I will recognize him by your description.

Sincerely,
Corinne Edwards

Dear Sheila,

How do I know I am falling in love with him?

All I can tell you is that one day I looked into his eyes and I felt like I was looking into my own. I feel like I have known him for centuries and that he is me and I am him.

I can tell he really likes me and yet he makes no moves toward me. Just friends.

Don't ask what's happened to me. I have lost my mind.

Nuts in Chicago,
Corinne

Henri Bendel
New York

Mail to: Henri Bendel
PO BOX 000000
COLUMBUS OH 00000-0000

CORINNE EDWARDS
CHICAGO, IL 00000-0000

New balance: $522.63

Minimum payment due:

Please pay by:

↑ DETACH HERE ↑

↑ DETACH HERE ↑

Keep this part for your records.

How we figured what you owe on your ACCOUNT NO.

Date	Charges ■ Payment ■ Credits	Amount
LINGERIE		$522.63

Smoke Screen

How do I tell him
he doesn't love me as a sister?
You don't tell your sister
you like going to the grocery store with her.

I have a brother
who likes me a lot.
He never looks at me like that,
with lights in his eyes,
corners crinkled in delight.

How do I tell him
you don't tell your sister
how at home you feel with her,
and close, safe to share feelings,

and brothers don't hug sisters
those extra seconds
when everyone is saying good-bye,
or kiss them three times on the face,
instead of a peck on the cheek
and a rabbit punch in the arm.

How do I tell him
you don't tell your sister
how intense her eyes are,
how beautiful she looks—

How do I tell him,
and if I don't tell him,
how long
will it take him
to know?

E-mail:

Dear Paul and Peter—

Alex is the tattletale, as usual! I'm glad I don't have to pay your phone bills anymore.

He told you about Joseph! Did he also tell you that he is crazy about him? He is over here all the time talking to him.

On the other hand . . . I'm trying to figure out if he's a little jealous because I'm interested in someone or if he's jealous that his mother is taking up too much discussion time with his idol! Joseph has a Ph.D. in, you guessed it, philosophy. Alex thinks he is brilliant, and of course, he is.

It is nice for me that Alex approves of my new love interest. You know how he's always been before with any other man who walked in my door.

I can't wait for you to meet Joseph on your next trip to Chicago. He will fit right in (if all this works out) because he can wisecrack with the best of you characters. He's one of several boys in his family so he's had lots of practice in sparring!

Nothing has been discussed about long-term, but we are really getting close to each other and we have a lot in common. So far it is just a deep friendship. But what a nice way to start. It is also a little scary. I never thought I'd feel this way about a man again. But so sweet. And he is such fun.

Hope all is well with you guys in La-La Land! I loved the tape of your new band, Peter. They sound great. Keep up the good work. One of these days there will be a record deal! In the meantime, it is nice that you say you LOVE your job at the law firm.

Sending lots of love, as always—
Mom

Dear Junie Bug,

I am going to pass on our annual "Big Apple Experience" next month. The new plays are tempting, but I don't want to leave Chicago right now.

Joseph has been staying with me on and off for the past month because he has been depressed. So I want to be available in case he needs me.

He had a difficult childhood and has lost several members of his family just recently. That's enough to put anyone down. I know what loss is all about.

So I want to support him. You know, I never really had a male friend before. It is wonderful! We talk for hours and are so close.

I know you will understand. Joseph needs a lot of love right now. And June, I love him. He is family.

There will be lots of "Big Apples" for us in the future!

Much love to you,
Corinne

Present Tense

I cannot make up
all the love you have missed.
I am only one person.
I cannot be your mother, father,
the friends who abandoned you,
teachers who programmed their beliefs,
dogmas which stunted your growth.

I cannot go back to beginnings,
pick you up when you scraped your knee,
rock you to sleep when your dog died,
comfort a teenager's sadness.
I've just arrived.

I've entered the scene too late
to offer advice
on past tense decisions,
cradle you when you lost hope,
be your champion,
support you unconditionally
no matter what you became.

I can only be here today,
another war victim, a wounded child,
carrying the load of my defeats,
limping alongside,
too proud to ask for assistance,
needing you to be here for me.

I cannot make up
all the love you have missed.
I am only one person.
There is no going back.
But if you will reach out your hand,
I can love you now.

E-mail:

Dear Paul, Peter, and Alex—

Okay—I know that you are all mad at me for canceling my air reservation to Los Angeles for Thanksgiving and that Alex had to come alone.

I'm sorry that it happened the way it did at the last minute, but I had no idea that Joseph was going to go into such a deep depression this week. How can I leave a person who means so much to me when he is in such distress? He is just sitting there with his head in his hands. And he needs me.

The fact that I care so much about Joseph does not mean I don't love you boys and that our family time is not important. I hope you realize that. But try to see it this way. You three have each other. He has nowhere to go. I just could not leave him in the condition he is in. It's not like I could pop over and have dinner with you and then come home. You're in California, two thousand miles away. I would have been abandoning him for a long, lonely weekend.

Don't let this spoil your time with each other. You always have so much fun together. And please understand that I am with you in spirit. I miss being with you as much as you were counting on my being there.

There will be many other Thanksgivings when Joseph will be out of this phase and part of the family, celebrating with all of us.

This is a very important relationship to me. Please try to understand that.

I love you all and will speak with you (probably several times) tomorrow.

Your devoted (in spite of the way it looks to you right now)—
Mom

Premarital Contract

- All 100 percent cotton shirts go to the laundry
- You take the shirts and pick them up
- Gamble with money I don't know about
- When you lose, don't tell me
- Don't cheat on me
- If you cheat on me, never admit it, even if the hotel has billed for two breakfasts
- If we have an argument, remember we are two eloquent people
- Never be silent for more than twenty-four hours
- We must have a permanent residence somewhere
- Let me see my old friends alone
- Know that neatness is one of my character defects
- Be nice to my boring relatives
- Don't use sex as a weapon
- When I'm quiet, it's me, not you
- Try to like my kids
- Pack your own suitcases
- Never forget you are my best friend
- Don't threaten me with leaving
- Don't ever leave

Dear Sheila,

I put the travel agency on the market. Suddenly, I had no energy for it.

Listen to this scenario. After thinking about it for a year, I woke up one morning, got a cup of coffee, was reading the paper—not thinking about business—looked up, and decided, *I'm listing the agency today.* That was that. It's funny how we mull things over and over then make up our minds in one second.

A couple of people are already interested. They all want to know why I am selling such a good agency, and I wish I could give them a sensible answer. Should I say, "It was fun, but it's over?" The truth would really confuse them. I don't think they would understand that I have run all over the world trying to get happy, and I'm tired of the chase. I haven't found peacefulness anywhere.

I have to find this peace. I don't know where it is, but I do know where it is not. It is not outside of me—who I'm with, where I go, what I do, or where I live.

I admit, I am afraid. The travel business has been my life for a long time. I don't want to go back on my decision, but I also don't know what I am going to do with the rest of my life. What's next? I guess I have to concentrate on trusting that the next step will be shown to me in the proper time. Whatever it is.

Love to you, Sheila,
Corinne

P.S. The "romance" is stumbling along. I don't understand that either.

Sesame Street

In the travel business,
you get some odd requests.

A client called—routine—
except—
he wanted to bring a bird
to a funeral in Florida.

His cousin loved the bird.
It was an only child.
They had lived together
for a long time.

"A bird? No problem.
Put him in a box with holes.
No one will even know he's on the plane!"

The bird is rather large.
I said, "How big?"
(It sounded like a Bob Newhart joke.)
"The size of a chicken?"
And too valuable to put in baggage.

A rare bird.
To a funeral in Florida.
Carried in the cabin.
With the passengers.
Turned out it even talked.

We have to help each other.

E-mail:

Dear Paul and Peter—

In my wondering what I was going to be when I grow up, it suddenly occurred to me that you are all supporting me in selling the travel agency and doing whatever I want to do with my life!

And I realized that I am getting a payback from all of you for always allowing you to do whatever you want with your lives (with only a minimum of motherly interference!).

I just called Alex to thank him. And I want to thank the California crowd too.

Gratefully and with love—
Mom

P.S. Speaking of interfering, Peter. The firm's offer to subsidize your law school should be considered very seriously. Music will be with you for your whole life. You will always find pleasure in it. But I know you will make the right decision.

Dear Joseph,

You said the other day that you thought letters were some-times more expressive than conversations, so I am writing to explain what you must consider a change in my behavior these past few months.

You mentioned once that you remember vividly the first time you saw me on the last day of the seminar we both attended. So do I.

You walked toward me and I saw LIGHTS all around you. It flashed through my mind, *Oh, here he is. Why didn't I see him before?*

Of course, I immediately pushed that thought out of my mind. Thought I was crazy. I didn't even know your name, and for all I knew, you were there with a wife. You were a stranger.

During the next year, I grew to love you as a friend. Looking back on the beginning, I admit that I looked for-ward eagerly to seeing you, cared about you, liked you to hug me—and you made me laugh! We had a lot of fun together. I have always trusted you and feel that I've known you forever. Which is probably why I can write this letter.

Everything changed the day you were sick and I took you to the doctor. I was bustling around your house, getting ready to leave. You were sitting in your big chair. A poor sick guy. I walked over and kissed you good-bye. I looked into your eyes and I felt like lightning had hit me! *My God,* I thought, *I am in love with this man.*

It threw me for a loop. I didn't expect it. You did not fit my profile. But it was true. It is true.

I have never been in love with a best friend before. It is even possible that I have never been in love before. It feels nice. It feels safe. I know you would not knowingly hurt me.

Being this honest is a big leap for me. And this letter may be a shock to you. But I am not afraid of you although you said recently that you do not know if you are ready for a relationship. That struck me as odd since we already have one.

So if this same realization ever dawns on you, I'd like to be with you. Every day. One day at a time. This may be the best offer you have ever had.

You've taught me a lot about what unconditional love is. So, always know that I wish you your highest good—even if it is not me.

Love always,
Corinne

Retailers National Bank an affiliate of

Marshall Fields

ACCOUNT NUMBER	MINIMUM DUE	NEW BALANCE	AMOUNT PAID
		$ 372.42	

INDICATE AMT ABOVE

ADDRESS _____

CITY _____ ST. ____ ZIP _____

PHONE # _____

PLEASE INDICATE ANY
ADDRESS OR PHONE #
CHANGES ABOVE

RETAILERS NATIONAL BANK
PO BOX 00000
MINNEAPOLIS, MN 00000-0000

CORINNE H EDWARDS
CHICAGO, IL 00000-0000

mail this portion with your payment

LUXURY SHEETS AND PILLOWCASES

$372.42

Monday

Another week without him.
It's Monday.
It stretches out like a desert
without a tree,
followed by Tuesday, Wednesday,

after a weekend of fantasies,
looking out the one-way glass
of the front door.
His car will be passing.
He is still deciding.

Get the makeup on quickly.
He is arriving!
I've come to ask you to marry me.
When? Now. Today.

His mother has died. He needs me.
Calls for help. For comfort.
Stay there. I'll be there in a half hour.

The navy dress for the funeral.
Pale pink for the wedding.
The bags are packed a dozen times.

Pushing myself out the door
to shop for a bathing suit I don't need.
Leaving explicit information about the store.
In case of emergency.
In case he wants me.
Checking the dress rack for something nice
in pale pink.

Maybe Thursday he will call.

Another week without him.

a life without him

Wasting Time

It doesn't matter if he is exactly what you want.
(He's not ready to want you.)

Don't count that he makes your heart pound.
(He's not pounding on your door.)

Or explain he is just afraid of love.
(He isn't loving you.)

Expensive vigil.
Clocks are ticking
through months of yearning,

while somewhere,
someone
is searching furiously for you,
dreaming of you,
hungering for you,

waiting for you
to be free.

Dear kids in the office,

Tahiti is the most beautiful place I have ever been. It is the South Pacific we have pictured in our dreams.
    See you soon.

Love,
Corinne

Escape

Run away,
run away
to a magic isle,
where a crystal sea
unwinds at the feet
of volcanoes.

Race ahead of regret
before thoughts pursue.
Distance the sorrow.

Blot bitter tears with snow white sand.
Lance the loss with shooting stars.
Let the rainbows paint reality.

Run so far away,
so far away,
that your mind,
your heart, your breaking heart,
can't find you.

Dear Sheila,

I know I haven't written for a few months but I have been in a terrible state of grieving. I really did a number on myself. I wrote a letter to Joseph telling him I was in love with him and it ruined everything.

He was very sweet, but he said he just wanted to be friends. After all, it is not as though he didn't warn me he wasn't ready for a relationship. But I wasn't so nice. We had some nasty words. Mostly mine. Everything they say about a woman scorned is true.

Then I tried to recoup my pride by saying of course we would be friends, but everything changed. I probably should have let things go on the way they were. Maybe he would have fallen in love with me in time without my pushing it.

Perhaps, if I wait, things will change and he will see it differently. Otherwise, I don't know if I can just be his friend. It is so painful to love someone who doesn't love you back. This is the first man I have been interested in since Julie died and it is a devastating disappointment. It's a much different kind of grief when someone dies. It is done. You can't get them back. You finally have to settle for it. With Joseph there is always that tormenting hope that something can still happen. That he will come to his senses and see how good we are together.

I am trying to get my head together. I am a woman with grown kids who are off on their own. It is undignified to feel this way at my age.

Love,
Corinne

P.S. The travel agency may be sold.

Retailers National Bank an affiliate of

Marshall Fields

ACCOUNT NUMBER	MINIMUM DUE	NEW BALANCE	AMOUNT PAID
		$ 0.00	

INDICATE AMT ABOVE

ADDRESS

CITY   ST.   ZIP

PHONE #

PLEASE INDICATE ANY
ADDRESS OR PHONE #
CHANGES ABOVE

RETAILERS NATIONAL BANK
PO BOX 00000
MINNEAPOLIS, MN 00000-0000

CORINNE H EDWARDS
CHICAGO, IL 00000-0000

mail this portion with your payment

LUXURY SHEETS AND PILLOWCASES

$372.42

Dear Joseph,

Thanks for your call yesterday when you asked if I would be interested in producing "A Spiritual Seminar at Sea," with you as the guest lecturer.

It sounds like a wonderful idea and I am sure it will be very successful, but I've thought it over and I don't want to do it. I don't think it is in my best interest.

I've been more honest with you than any other man in my life, so I may as well not stop now. I love you, Joseph. I don't want to be your producer. I don't want you as a sometime roommate. I can't be just your friend. I want to be your wife and make a home with you.

I've been alone for five years now and I want to be a wife. Although it does not seem to me now that I could ever love anyone else but you, my rational mind keeps reminding me that this is not so. The truth is that there is someone else I can love in this universe. Somewhere. Sometime.

But for this to be possible—in order for me to heal and to get over wanting only you—I just can't see you at all. I can't have any contact with you. And if you don't think this is as hard as cutting off my right arm, you are wrong. In realizing this as my only option, I am also giving up my best friend and companion. It is an excruciatingly painful loss.

My plan was to let things be and do as you suggested— just remain friends. But when I examined my feelings more closely, being friends translated as you giving a little and me giving a lot. I want a fuller relationship with a beloved.

I have chastised myself for not being a big enough person

to be only friends, and perhaps that is true. But staying in contact with you ignites too much secret hope that you will suddenly realize you love me.

I don't doubt the sincerity of your feelings of friendship and caring for me, so I know you will be sad to lose me too. I ask forgiveness for any pain my decision causes you. But this is what I have to do. I have to take care of me. Please understand.

You will have no trouble finding another travel agent to produce your seminar. I wish you all the best with it.

And I wish you all the best in *every* part of your life. Good-bye, Joseph. Good luck. I'm moving on . . .

I'll always love you.

Corinne

Dear Sheila,

Because it was near Christmas, I decided to surprise you with a phone call to Korea. The operator was told that you had been transferred to Germany and was given the number of the Enlisted Men's Center. I can't understand why you would leave without letting me know.

There was a lot of confusion about where you were when the operator reached Germany, so I decided to talk to the person who answered. He said a plane with many young servicemen coming home for the holidays had crashed on the way to the United States. Later in the day, it was all over the news. He said you left right afterward. You told everyone you were not coming back. No one knew where you had gone.

Sheila, I can imagine how you feel. You must have been personally involved with many of them. They must represent a hundred sons to you.

I want to support you. You have done so much for me. Please don't deprive me of comforting you.

Sheila, you can't keep running from place to place. The grief of losing a son doesn't just go away. You don't absorb a loss like that. Let me help you. Please come stay with me for a while.

I am mailing this letter to the headquarters of the USO in Washington. I hope they will be able to forward it to you.

Please, please contact me.

I love you, Sheila, and treasure our friendship.

Corinne

Mr. Henry McBride
McBride, Coker and Klein

FROM: Corinne Edwards

PAGES: One

Dear Henry,

Regarding the latest glitch in the sale of Edwards Travel:

From what I understand, the buyer's attorney wants me to pay the Illinois franchise tax on the sale, and because there is no such tax on travel agencies in Illinois, you will not put it in the contract.

Henry, you are a wonderful friend and a great lawyer and I know that you just want to protect me, BUT FOR GOD'S SAKE PUT IT IN THE CONTRACT! I am willing to pay a tax that does not exist. Let's not lose the war here.

Also, even though our attorneys are negotiating, I had dinner last night with our buyers. I agreed to be a consultant for a year instead of six months. Don't get mad. Just include it in the contract.

With this new information, I am looking forward to the successful conclusion of this sale on Wednesday.

Fondest regards,
Corinne

Dearest Paul and Peter—

I was so consoled by the beautiful letters you both wrote to me about the breakup with Joseph. I felt so supported and loved when I read them. And Alex has been dropping by every day to see if I am okay.

I'm afraid this one is going to take time. It is as though I have lost a member of the family. I had high hopes that at last I had found a person to share my life. I know that you realize I've been lonely these past few years. It would be nice to have a partner again.

But I guess he was just not the one. It must be interesting to you to see that older people—even your Mom—can have her heart broken. These things do not seem to be age sensitive.

Of course I am going to be okay. How could I not be when I have three wonderful men like my sons in my corner all the time?

Thank you again for your loving letters—

All my love to you both,
Mom

Out for Lunch

"No, I can't have lunch," I'll say.
"Some other time.
I'm booked today."
Too busy piecing up a heart.
After all these months,
it's still apart.

"It's not a good idea," I'll say.
You're in my thoughts all through the day.
"We can't be friends. Not now. Not yet."
I dream you have not gone away.

"I'm really tied up now," I'll say.
"A lot is going on," I lie.
Replacement parts are hard to find.
I would see your face and start to cry.

"No, I can't have lunch," I'll say.
Feels like you left me yesterday.

To sit so close and not to touch—

It's much too soon for us to lunch.

Dear New Travel Agents!

Well, we did it! In spite of our lawyers fighting over terms we had already agreed on, the sale of Edwards Travel Advisors to you has been completed.

I wish you all the luck and enjoyment I had with the agency for so many years. It will be an exciting business for you.

Please know that I am available, past the date shown in the contract, for any help or advice you may need along the way. I am so pleased that you are keeping all the staff. Those kids in the office really run it anyway.

Break a leg!

All the best,
Corinne

Moments

Why is it
when I stare backward
on the landscape of my life,
the only signposts still standing
are the losses?

Where are the moments?
Always waiting, waiting for things,
for children to start school,
mortgages to be paid,
for Christmas, summer,
marriages to begin,
to be over.

Or rushing, out of breath,
I have slammed so many doors,
missed friendships,
meeting obligations, making deadlines,
stretching to goals that meant nothing.

I can't wait anymore
to hear the ocean while I sleep,
for the glass table which is too expensive,
a screened porch.
A man who adores me.

I want to run along a beach with no destination,
read all day long in my nightgown,
throw away my eyeliner.

I want to fall madly in love with an unsuitable person.
Forever is not so long anymore.

I want to live,
so if I ever look back again,
I'll remember the moments.

Dear Sheila,

It was such a relief to get your long letter after all these months and to hear that you are well and enjoying the small town in which you've chosen to live. It must be beautiful in the mountains.

I do understand that you need to take this time to be alone. If you want to talk about it in the future, I am available. In the meantime, I am just so happy to hear from you. I think you are right when you say that the healing benefits of isolation are undervalued. I've been doing a lot of isolating and healing and reading too.

In answer to your questions, I'll bring you up-to-date on my life.

The new owners of the travel agency are enjoying the business. They've asked me to continue working with a few of my more demanding clients so I still have my hand in, without all the responsibility of the everyday operation. It suits me fine, and it takes up the slack while I am deciding what I want to be when I grow up. When people ask me what I do, I tell them I am "a recovering entrepreneur."

I am glad to report that I am healing from my disappointing love affair. Joseph was a remarkable lesson for me—and one that was necessary so I could get in touch with what I want in a relationship. He was an important teacher. It boils down to one crystal clear revelation: *Why in the world would I want a man who doesn't want me?*

I've been fascinated with a book I'm reading on relationships, especially by one of the suggestions to establish a "bottom line" in all areas of life. The author advises that we decide not what we want, but what we CANNOT DO WITH-OUT—whether it is in business or in personal relationships. An interesting distinction! He goes on to say that once we establish these minimum requirements—not frills, but basic needs—we must refuse to compromise them. In love relationships, these are especially important. It seems what most of us do is recognize the unacceptable right away but go ahead and hope for the best to happen. Of course, it rarely does.

The author gave an example from his own life. He said that he loves to ski, and at first, he put this on his list as a bottom-line requirement of the woman he hoped to meet. Then he realized it was a preference, not a necessity. A necessity for him is that she is monogamous, doesn't drink, and wants to marry and have a home and children.

Well, it set me to thinking about what I cannot do without in a relationship. I'm still working on it, but for openers, there are three things:

1. That he is monogamous. He may have women friends, but I am the center of his life. (One of my friends says she wants a man who wakes up every morning and says, "Thank God she's in my life!" That's about right.)
2. That my happiness, feelings, and welfare are as important to him as his own.

   And—surprise!

3. That he is a home-hearth kind of guy who wants a quiet, orderly, and peaceful life. (No, I haven't given up travel entirely, but I have discovered I am a domestic animal. Making a big pot of soup on a cold day gives me pleasure. I like to plant tulip bulbs and know I'll be there to see them come up in the spring. I am happy at home!)

I am tempted to add a lot of other things to this list, but I want to make sure they are part of the rock-bottom basic package. And I have some more profound thinking to do in discovering my "bottom line" about work and where I want to live permanently. That's my next project.

Maybe this would be an interesting exercise for you to try with all the decisions you want to make now.

The other book I am involved in is *A Course in Miracles*. You may remember I joined a study group awhile back. It is teaching me that we came to this world to learn lessons, and the teaching is exactly where we are now. Even misery is on our program in order for us to grow. No one and no thing is in our lives by chance.

We go through a lot of pain through our refusal to accept where someone else is on his or her journey. We think if we love a person enough, he or she will change. We don't trust that everyone knows what to do. All people change on their own schedules. How much easier everything would be if we really got that. It takes a building falling on our heads to make us give up the control we never had in the first place!

So, Sheila, that's what's happening in my life. What an interesting time it has been for both of us in the past few years! Thanks for sharing my voyage and letting me share yours. What would I do without your advice, your ear, and your support? We really need our friends. Especially our women friends. Who else can understand us and put up with us as well as other women?

Please take very good care of yourself and keep in touch. And with all the soul-searching you are doing, I hope you are remembering all the people you have touched and helped—and who love you—from all over the world.

Including your pen pal,
Corinne

Endless Love

The pain is gone.
The giant tear I clutched,
uncried,
has leaked away.

Only the love is real.
It shimmers in my mind
like a golden sun at dawn.

Our arguments, the jealousies,
imagined treasons, bitter words,
have all dissolved

and only tender memories remain—

of gentle mornings,
football games,
meals prepared and cleared away—
the tuneless songs you hum,
and prayers we prayed.

No accidental joining ours!
A collision caused in time!
A karmic roller-coaster ride!

With hairpin turns
and high sky dives!

But now at last,
peace has arrived.
Explosions gone.
The walls thrown up in fear
have tumbled down.

And now—

no longer blind,
my heart can find
the quiet,
endless love
you are
inside.

Dearest Junie Bug,

Thanks for sending the twenty pictures of Danielle. You are right. She is beautiful! I am so jealous that you beat me to it!

I smiled several times when I read your letter about how brilliant this child already is at one month old. I kept remembering your statement that you were not going to be ONE OF THOSE GRANDMOTHERS! But that's okay. We'll let you. I'll be so happy to meet our infant wonder when I come in next week for our "Big Apple Experience!"

I have also been thinking a lot about our long, philosophical conversation on the phone a few days ago, when we did all that analyzing and comparing of our lives.

One thing you said has been going around and around in my mind. You commented, "You have had such a full life. You haven't missed a thing!"

I decided you are wrong. I've missed a lot of things. Even though you minimize that you stayed home and raised six children, you have had a very full life. You always had a grip on who you are and what you came into this world to do. I've been running on remote control.

Our conversation has inspired me to go over all the things I have learned in the past years of being on my own. I feel I've grown so much, and I'd like to share these thoughts with you. I want to write them down. Perhaps clarify them for myself. So settle in. This is liable to be one of my long letters.

I don't want to invalidate my whole experience, but most of the time, I was the reflection of whoever or whatever was in front of me. With all my "independence," I made decisions that were colored by the opinions of others. It was a new and surprising question to stop and ask, "What's best for you in this situation? What do you want here?" At first I drew a blank. I didn't know what I wanted. I was so used to using the "right thing" as a measure, or at least, presenting a face I thought would be liked and approved. I didn't allow myself to know myself. I wasn't aware there was someone to know.

Now I am seeing that all this is part of a sacred journey. And the destination is knowing that we can only be happy by giving full rein to being ourselves and using our creative abilities. Not holding back. Whether we are running a business or nursing a baby.

I've wondered why it takes so much time, soul searching, and heartbreak to remind us of such a simple truth. It seems we need pain to wake us up—to make us grow—to give us confidence to trust the real and loving person inside of us.

At first, you feel a little like Humpty-Dumpty because it is scary and new to live honestly with your true nature—to be your authentic self. It takes courage to feel what you feel, say what you think, and ask for what you want. But you know what? This is a nice person to be around. The mask has been dropped. Suddenly, when you least expect it, you become someone who is whole—someone who can accept love and who can love back.

We women of this century have had a difficult time with this. The pendulum has swung from our being dependent on men all the way to our trying to be men. The middle ground is to recognize and use our unique qualities—our intuition and power as women. Our inherent talents for compassion, giving, and forgiving are invaluable, whether we use them in personal relationships or in the business world. The same ability we exercise in nurturing a family can be used in the money game.

There is a revolution happening in the business world today. The wave is toward win-win on all sides. Cheating is out. I saw a sales seminar advertised recently. The theme was "Stop selling! Start helping!" This is second nature to women. We could teach men a thing or two about helping and serving. We have finally come into style in business. They need us.

Those of us who have caught on to this can reach back and help our sisters to know their value. A thirty-year-old woman knows something the twenty-five-year-old can use. Men have always helped each other with their good ol' boy network. We can learn from them.

Your life, June, is an inspiration to women with families. You have raised children with dignity and grace. There are women who are hungry to learn what you have to teach them about parenting. Some of us can lead women in combining home and family with business careers. But at whatever stage we are, there is someone who needs to know what we know.

I still would like to be married, to have a life partner again, but it has gotten to be more a preference than a need. I've talked a lot about women supporting women but all of us are in this together. It is about men and women celebrating our differences—loving and accepting each other just the way we are. Encouraging each other to be the best we can be whether we are driving a bus or composing an opera.

I believe I will marry because it is on my agenda, and I am much more clear about what I want now. And if you truly want something, you will get it. The man for me knows who he is and I have to allow him the time and responsibility of finding me. But he is not the only item on my schedule. At the top of the list is to remember to enjoy and relish every minute of this very day—to use it up, get every drop of experience out of it. It is the capacity I have—right now—to live in this moment and no other. It is the only time I have and it is here. It is pregnant with possibility. I have squandered years in wishing, hoping, and planning for things in the future. I have taken for granted or ignored the joy that was right in my hands. I had a lot of fun I didn't know I was having until I looked back at it.

So, my sweet sister, those are the thoughts that are going through my head. I wonder if you know how precious our relationship has been to me. All through this learning, I could count on you as my sounding board. Always there—never judging—and willing to let me change my mind, without ever saying, "But you said . . ." You have worried all the worries, laughed all the laughs, and cried all the tears right beside me. Your friendship is a rare gift.

I am looking forward to seeing you at our next "Big Apple Experience." And I appreciate you getting the theater tickets as usual. My check is included here.

But of course this time is different because I will meet the first of the new generation of women in our family. The main event this time is Danielle.

I hope you are prepared to share her because I can't wait to get my hands on that baby!

Your devoted sister,
Corinne

E-mail:

Dearest Paul,

I was so by surprised by your announcement on the telephone this morning that I don't remember what I said to you. You said that YOU ARE GETTING MARRIED!

I have to get used to this. With the two million or so women who have gone through your revolving door, the "M" word has never been mentioned before (at least not by YOU). But of course, the right one did not arrive until now. I am so happy for you.

When you brought Debra over to visit at Christmas, I remembered her well. You dated her girlfriend in high school and she was part of the crowd. I always liked her. Imagine your meeting her back in Chicago after fifteen years.

As I got over the shock today, I started to feel ecstatic! Debra fills your criteria of being blond, beautiful, and blue-eyed—but she is the legendary "girl next door" a mother dreams about for her son! And both of your brothers are so approving and pleased.

So, my darling Paul, congratulations! I am delighted for you and for Debra, and for me. Just think! I will finally have a daughter. I can't wait to hear the date. And when can I call her parents? We all have to meet. And I have to talk to Debra about the colors she is planning so we can think about dresses and all. Aunt June and I have to shop. So many happy plans to make.

It seems like only good things are happening in the family now. With Alex's graduation with honors coming up and Peter considering law school and now a wedding! Your Dad must be up in heaven smiling.

I feel so blessed! Thank you for finding Debra again.

You are going to have a wonderful marriage!

Much, much love from your—
Mom

Split Screen

There is no more little girl.
She grew up.
Quietly.
Right beside the fraudulent life you created,
the one that struggles, is unhappy.

You do not permit the grown-up girl to be.

She is kept on the sidelines,
watching your games,
while you pretend protection.
You locked her up—
even denied she existed.

I don't need protection!
I'm a big girl now!
Whole. Real.
I've seen it all—
the mess you've made!
Been alert, vigilant.
Learned.
Mourned the time you've wasted!

The person you manufactured is the frightened one.

I'm not afraid.
Let me out!
You never let me make mistakes.
Set me free!
I may get hurt.
But I'm not as fragile as you think.

And if I have to make
a new life,
have new friends, or fall in love—
let me try.

You've done a lousy job.

Go away.
Let me.

Irish Doctor Wanted

You are a mature, healthy, available man—attractive, dedicated, vital—still yearning for that special companion—and probably too busy to find her. I am a fit, trim lady of a certain age, still very pretty—great smile—open heart—a cook—bookworm—nice. Take the time. Make the call.

About the Author

Corinne Edwards has traveled several life paths—from business owner to sales trainer, author, lecturer, poet, and TV producer. She is the author of two other books, *Low Pain Threshold* and *Love Waits on Welcome . . . And Other Miracles.*

In her business incarnation, she was one of the first women to be invited into Rotary International and to serve as a chairperson of a chamber of commerce in the United States. She was also president of a chapter of the American Cancer Society.

In recent years, her focus has shifted to the area of personal growth and human potential. Edwards has conducted self-esteem classes based on the principles of love and forgiveness in *A Course in Miracles* in Cook County Jail. Her program for rehabilitation for prostitutes was one of the first of its kind in the country.

Currently she produces and hosts *Book Tours . . . with Corinne Edwards* for Wisdom Television.

For more information about Corinne Edwards, visit her Web site at www.awomanalone.com.

Hazelden Transitions is an initiative between Hazelden Foundation's Information and Educational Services division and Transitions Bookplace, Inc.

Hazelden Information and Educational Services helps individuals, families, and communities prevent and/or recover from alcoholism, drug addiction, and other related diseases and conditions. We do this by partnering with authors and other experts to deliver information and educational products and services that customers use to aid their personal growth and change, leading along a wholistic pathway of hope, health, and abundant living. We are fortunate to be recognized by both professionals and consumers as the leading international center of resources in these areas.

Transitions Bookplace, Inc., founded in Chicago, Illinois, in 1989, has become the nation's leading independent bookseller dedicated to customers seeking personal growth and development. Customers can choose from more than thirty thousand books, videos, pamphlets, and musical selections. Authors appear frequently for special events or workshops in the Transitions Learning Center. Also available in the store is a legendary collection of exquisite international gifts celebrating body, mind, and spirit.

This Hazelden Transitions Bookplace initiative is dedicated to all brave souls who seek to change courses in their lives, their families, and their communities in order to achieve hope, health, and abundant living.

Transitions Bookplace
1000 West North Avenue
Chicago, IL 60622
312-951-READ
800-979-READ
www.transitionsbookplace.com

Hazelden Information and Educational Services
15251 Pleasant Valley Road
Center City, MN 55012-0176
800-328-9000
www.hazelden.org